THE BESWICK PRICE GUIDE
BY HARVEY MAY

ACKNOWLEDGEMENTS

My thanks are due to my publishers Kevin Pearson and Francis Salmon whose efforts have, once again, made this project worthwhile.
Thanks are also due to my wife, Hazel, for her constant help and support in putting this book together.

Harvey May

Cover photograph: Francis Salmon. Other photographs, Trevor Leak/Norman Jones, Gordon Clark Publicity Ltd, Lawrence Baker and Glynis and Pete.

Important Notice

All the information contained in this book has been compiled from reliable sources and every effort has been made to eliminate errors. Neither the publishers nor the authors can be held responsible for losses which may occur in the purchase, sale or other transaction of items because of the information contained herein. Readers who feel they have discovered errors are invited to write and inform us so that these may be corrected in subsequent editions.

Typeset by E J Folkard, Crayford, Kent
Printed in England by Colourset Litho Limited, Croydon
Produced by Francis Salmon
Compiled by James Scannell

To my grandsons
Jack and Joshua
who also have a
small Beswick collection

About the Author

Harvey May was born in Wood Green, London in 1932, the son of a Durham miner who had moved to London after the General Strike of 1926. During the war years he was a child evacuee moving from London to the country town of Halstead, Essex. After the interruption of the war years Harvey finished his education at Enfield Technical School and left there to start work in 1949. He married Hazel in 1954 and moved to his present home in Essex in 1958. He has two sons, both married, and three grandsons, who each have their own growing collections.

His first interest in any hobby was the modest but popular schoolboy pastime of collecting bus and train numbers, an interest which took him far and wide on similarly modest transport — his bike!

In 1952 Harvey joined British Railways as Technical Assistant in the Civil Engineer's Office at King's Cross station, but has now retired from the railway. Throughout this time he has amassed a collection of railway items and many related books.

China and crested ware have always been an area of interest for Harvey and it was the chance purchase of a Beswick Penguin in 1980 which led to a large collection and the quest for information.

The results of his efforts lie between the covers of this book, to be enjoyed by equally enthusiastic collectors.

Contents

AN INTRODUCTION

From the Author

Welcome to this second edition of the *Beswick Collectors Price Guide*.

Model details are again presented in the same form as the first edition and you will be able to identify most pieces without any difficulty.

Each section has been updated with the latest available information and all new and withdrawn models have been listed up to January 1992.

There has been a considerable change in the marketing strategy of Royal Doulton during the last two years and this has led to backstamp changes which have dismayed many collectors and confused the majority of dealers.

Top favourites in the Beswick range are the Beatrix Potter figures and since being introduced in 1947 they have carried various styles of backstamp.

From 1st August, 1989 however, the backstamp has changed to Royal Albert, even though all models are still made in the Beswick factory.

This has led to considerable resistance by collectors, who now only look for models which carry the Beswick mark.

The other backstamp changes have had the effect of focusing attention on *all* pieces marked Beswick, whether current or not.

The following models, originally in the Beswick range, have been transferred to the Royal Doulton Series and a new DA (Doulton Animals) number has been allocated:

1) Connoisseur
2) Horses (all except 868, 1501 and 1730)
3) Foals
4) "Fireside" Dogs and Cat
5) Old English Dogs (1378/3 to 1378/7)
6) Dogs (medium) 3055 and above
7) Spirit Dogs on plinth (matt)
8) "Good Companion" Dogs (2982 and above)
9) Cats

All now carry the Royal Doulton backstamp, and all are still made in the Beswick factory. Full details of the new DA and old Beswick numbers are given and should help identification.

There now remain 109 models in the current Beswick price list which carry the Beswick backstamp. This compares with 317 in 1986.

It really is very hard to follow the logic of these changes, with the need to prepare and print new price lists, design and manufacure new packaging and the publicity needed to ensure sales, it becomes questionable whether it will bring in sufficient new business to warrant the changes.

There are a large number of people who would favour at least a partial return to the Beswick mark, together with a recognition through advertising and publicity material, that the John Beswick Studio of Royal Doulton is still a force to be reckoned with.

Since publication of my *Beswick Collectors Handbook* in 1986, interest has spread in North America, Canada, Australia, New Zealand and South Africa and membership of the Beswick Collectors Circle is now over 400.

Beswick pieces are now appearing quite extensively on the secondary market and dealers are now well aware of the name. This increased awareness and interest has caused many prices to rise steeply. Many Doulton dealers now stock Beswick and for the last five years it has also been available at the Stafford Doulton Fair, held in June.

Collectors are quite mystified by those models which form part of a set, have been in production for a number of years and yet are almost impossible to find. Three possible explanations are:

1) Production difficulties resulting in fewer becoming available.
2) In the case of earlier models, exports could have had priority.
3) Limited number of production runs.

Horses continue to create interest and uncertainty, due to the Beswick policy, up to the late 1960s, of offering many of them in up to six different decorations.

The wide variety of shapes and breeds, causes a great deal of confusion, especially when trying to be sure about which horse you have just bought!

The ideal solution would be for a shape guide to be made available so that identification is simplified.

A great deal of interest is being shown in the many variations which are coming to light. These are often not discovered until two different models of the same shape number are put together for comparison. There are also a fair number of colour variations turning up.

A recent discovery has been the appearance of several "look-alikes", which appear to be genuine Beswick, but are not. Pottery bases, impressed "Beswick England", are being used to mount unmarked cats and dogs from another pottery and these are being passed off as a genuine Beswick product.

Throughout the book a model which is still in production and marked 'C' in the lists, is priced at the Current Suggested Retail Selling price, including VAT at 17½%. Prices are taken from the January 1992 price list, published by Royal Doulton.

This leads me, once again, to remind you that all prices quoted are only a guide as to what you might expect to pay and you must always make your **own** decision as to how much you **actually** pay.

Collecting Beswick

Many people who attend antique fairs are merely there to look, to pick up pieces of bric-a-brac and odd items that catch the eye, wondering if there will be something which really captivates them enough to justify becoming a collector.

I was just such a visitor of fairs in the early 1980s when something really did catch my eye — a penguin with an orange umbrella over its head. It was such an amusing little model and I had to have it. It was my first Beswick purchase, sowing the seed of collector enthusiasm, and leading to further purchases.

As I began to build up a number of pieces and attend fairs simply to find Beswick, questions arose — "How many are there in the set?", "Who modelled this or that piece?", "When was it made?". There were few answers forthcoming from dealers who only put Beswick on their stalls because of its obvious quality. So began, not only the seeds of collecting, but also of research to find some answer to my many questions, not least of which was "Who are Beswick?", "When did they start?", "What makes them produce the things they do?"

The more I researched through old catalogues the more I became aware of the great diversity and range of Beswick from colourful Christmas tankards to the spectacular lifelike models of wild animals such as the African Elephant. The company has consistently produced excellent models of horses, dogs and wild animals, and is well established as a specialist in its field.

I believe some of the Beswick models to be truly magnificent. The Connoisseur Collection, in particular, represents the ultimate in artistic design and detail. The subjects range from award winning showdogs to famous racehorses such as Arkle. Standing in state on their mahogany plinths they take pride of place in the enthusiast's home.

The Beswick models are not only accurate and detailed, but they are appealing too! Humour is very much to the fore, as in the cat playing the violin or the happy mongrel dog with outrageously proportioned limbs and head. Even models not specifically intended to be funny are often engaging in their poses, and this certainly adds to the enjoyment of collecting.

The company has certainly stood the test of time and the basis of this success can be attributed mainly to the work of John Ewart and Gilbert Beswick who broke new ground in the thirties.

Art Director James Hayward also deserves special mention here because he had over thirty designers working under him during the period 1934 to 1969 when Royal Doulton took over the company and he continued to work for Beswick until his retirement in 1975.

Although the number of people collecting Beswick has been growing in recent years, enthusiasts and collectors have been hampered until now by a lack of detailed knowledge on the pieces produced. Nine years ago I decided to try and research further the history behind my Beswick collection and contacted the factory for further information. Very little was immediately accesssible but I was invited to examine the old pattern books. From these and other sources in the factory I have been able to trace the production details and history of Beswick's output since the 1930s.

I hope you will enjoy this book, your introduction to the world of Beswick collecting. No doubt you will form your own particular favourites from the wealth of choice available but some of the collecting tips below may be helpful.

One final word concerning the pronunciation of the Beswick name; the 'W' is clearly sounded and the phonetic spelling is therefore 'BES-WIK' and not 'BEZ-ZIK'.

Collecting Tips
and Valuing Discontinued Beswick

Once collectors become 'hooked' they often find it difficult to know when to stop buying and this can create all kinds of problems, particularly if the pieces are very expensive. Beswick wares are now very collectable and prices have risen steeply during the last two years. No longer is it possible to find relatively rare models at bargain prices. The number of possible collecting subjects is enormous though and the best way of starting is by choosing a specific theme such as 'horses', 'Shakespearian ware' or 'humorous subjects'.

This book gives details of the variety available, but it is a good idea to find out what the current price range is for the chosen pieces before embarking on an area which is too expensive. It is no good deciding to collect a particular series without knowing how many pieces there are and how much you are likely to have to spend to make a complete collection.

The only guide as to the value or worth of a particular piece is the amount that the collector is prepared to spend. As the market for Beswick develops (and it is developing at a tremendous rate), collectors will become more and more aware of which models are the hardest to find and, in accordance with the dictates of demand and supply, the prices of these are bound to rise more than the rest. This is what makes collecting so enjoyable, particularly the pleasure of a 'find' which is picked up at a reasonable price.

The collector will find this book useful for identifying models, their dates of production and withdrawal, but it must be noted that some of the pieces do not have the model number impressed on their base and that where the base is too small for the Beswick mark it may only have the 'England' stamp on it. In these cases the collector, coming across the model for the first time at an antiques fair, may not recognise it as Beswick. The

Page from 1946 catalogue

Selection of Wall birds from 1946 catalogue

Page from 1939 catalogue

Page from 1939 catalogue

368 324 317 696 397

286 454 721 398 302

497 617 88 360

568 383 569 618 453

450/1 369 316 323 315

663 665 698 692 450/2 697 624 664

Pages from a 1939 catalgoue

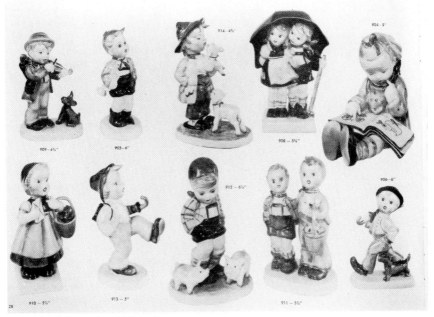

Hummel style figures from 1942 catalgoue

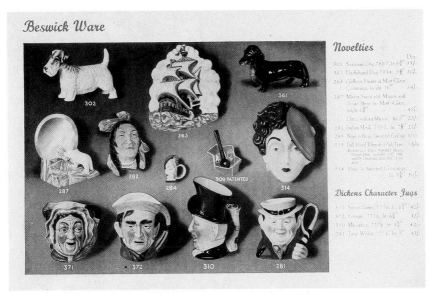

Page from pre-war catalogue illustrating 'novelties' and Dickens character jugs

difficulties involved in finding the final additions to a collection add to the pleasure of 'the hunt', which is, after all, what it is all about. GOOD HUNTING!

Identifying Marks and Model Numbers

Models are marked 'Beswick England', the exceptions being pieces which have small bases and are just stamped 'England'. The mark will either be impressed into or stamped onto the base or both!

Models, with sufficient room on the underside, will have impressed the name and number of the model.

The following mark variations will be found:

Selection of packing boxes

Rupert Bear's packing box

So far as is known every item produced since 1933 has been allocated a model number.

In some cases, for example wall mounted plaques of birds in flight, sets of different size models will be given the same number.

Colour variations also occur among animals and Dickens ware, with the same number applying each time. Many of the animals are available in either gloss or matt finish and some can be found with or without a china or wooden base. In all cases the same model number applies.

Decoration numbers containing four figures are hand painted on many of the older pieces. This is solely to identify the colour scheme used on a particular model and relates to the former practice of allowing purchasers of a particular model to choose from a range of colours. The retailer could then make an order on behalf of his customer, quoting the decoration number he wanted.

Dates of withdrawal are given where possible, though there can be a margin of a couple of years either side of the date given.

The following table gives the year of introduction for each model:

Year of Introduction

Numbers			Introduced	Numbers			Introduced
1	—	377	Undated				
378	—	460	1936	1921	—	1996	1964
461	—	567	1937	1997	—	2053	1965
568	—	672	1938	2054	—	2086	1966
673	—	794	1939	2087	—	2176	1967
795	—	880	1940	2177	—	2255	1968
881	—	968	1941	2256	—	2302	1969
969	—	990	1942	2303	—	2349	1970
991	—	1000	1943	2350	—	2396	1971
1001	—	1013	1944	2397	—	2443	1972
1014	—	1042	1945	2444	—	2500	1973
1043	—	1082	1946	2501	—	2522	1974
1083	—	1107	1947	2523	—	2554	1975
1108	—	1141	1948	2555	—	2582	1976
1142	—	1180	1949	2583	—	2607	1977
1181	—	1209	1950	2608	—	2636	1978
1210	—	1226	1951	2637	—	2666	1979
1227	—	1279	1952	2667	—	2700	1980
1280	—	1322	1953	2701	—	2750	1981
1323	—	1362	1954	2751	—	2804	1982
1363	—	1391	1955	2805	—	2846	1983
1392	—	1468	1956	2847	—	2899	1984
1469	—	1516	1957	2900	—	2960	1985
1517	—	1576	1958	2961	—	3031	1986
1577	—	1667	1959	3032	—	3114	1987
1668	—	1732	1960	3115	—	3179	1988
1733	—	1792	1961	3180	—	3225	1989
1793	—	1861	1962	3226	—	3275	1990
1862	—	1920	1963	3276	—	3330	1991
				3331	—		1992

Beswick Advertising Plaques

Beatrix Potter packing boxes

1052 *Barnacle Goose*

572 *Bird-in-Bush Plaque*

Part One: Animals

The name of Beswick is synonymous with meticulously faithful models of animals, whether they be horses, dogs, cattle, birds or fish. The appointment of Mr Arthur Gredington as modeller in 1939 was a major factor in the success of Beswick, for his original models were outstanding. When his skill was combined with that of mouldmaker, Arthur Hallam, and the patient attention and detail of the Beswick paintresses, the quality of the finished Beswick animal was assured.

Birds (All current birds carry a Beswick backstamp)

Many varieties and styles of birds are to be found in the Beswick collection. The earliest models are of a whimsical nature, such as the arrogant Penguin of 1936 modelled by Mr Owen. Later on in the 1930s it became fashionable to model birds in the form of wall plaques and today these are a very collectable series. Mr Watkin was the chief exponent of these particular ornaments and he followed his success with ducks by introducing sets of seagulls, pheasants and blue-tits in flight.

In contrast to the birds on the wing, Beswick artists also modelled a number of species of birds perched on boughs and tree trunks adorned with flowers and these were particularly popular in the forties. Until around 1965 the petals and leaves on the bases were modelled in high relief, but as these were vulnerable to damage they were subsequently replaced with hand-painted flowers in low relief.

During the 1950s the bird models became very stylised in the new stream-lined forms of the period. Kathi Urbach created two striking peacocks which could be used as containers for floral displays (1555 and 1556). Colin Melbourne also modelled some birds in the modern style, and these were known and marked as the "C.M." series and numbered in the "1400" range.

This artist was also responsible for the collection of decoy ducks (1518-1529) which were modelled from the birds sheltering in Peter Scott's sanctuary at Slimbridge. Jim Hayward was the Art Director at the time and he visited Peter Scott to select the species to be portrayed. The first three models in this set of twelve were produced in three sizes (see listing) but the remaining birds were made in one size only. These models are very collectable, and hard to find.

In recent years Graham Tongue has tended to work on the bird collection. To ensure that his models are accurate, he visits local aviaries and also the Natural History department of the City Museum and Art Gallery, Stoke-on-Trent, and the results of his research are evident in his studies for the Connoisseur range, the Golden Eagle (2062) and the Pheasant (2760). Since 1983 models have been available in either glossy or matt finish, with the exception of the Pheasant (2760).

L—R: **926** *Baltimore Orioles;* **929** *Chickadee;* **925** *Blue Jays*

L—R: **1226** *Pheasant;* **1022** *Doves;* **2078** *Pair of Pheasants;* **1219** *Jay;* **2063** *Pair of Grouse;* **1958** *Turkey;* **1218** *Green Woodpecker*

Model No	Name of Model	Height inches	Value £	Design Date	Withdrawn By
370	Three Ducks candle holder	3½	40-45	1935	1954
450/1	Penguin	8	60-65	1936	1955
450/2	Penguin	3½	40-45	1936	1955
465	Two Birds facing opposite ways on tree stumps	—	65-75	1937	1955
497	Pelican matchbox holder	4	30-35	1937	1955
572	Bird on bush plaque	7 x 4¼	65-75	1938	1954
574	Three Blue Tits plaque	9¾ x 5	65-75	1938	1955
617	Duck	—	30-35	1938	1955
618	Puffin	—	45-50	1938	1955
749	Mallard (rising)	6½	85-90	1939	1967
750	Mallard (settling)	6½	85-90	1939	1967
754	Pheasant ash tray	3½	10-15	1939	1971
755	Duck ash tray	4	10-15	1939	1969
756/1	Mallard	7	40-45	1939	1973
756/2	Mallard	5¾	25-30	1939	1973
756/2A	Mallard	4½	20-25	1939	1973
756/3	Mallard	3½	15-20	1939	1973
767	Pheasant (curved tail)	3	8-10	1939	1971
767	Pheasant (straight tail)	3	6·50	1971	C
768	Seagull	8½	100-150	1939	1955
769	Duck night-light holder	6	55-60	1939	1940
800	Penguin	2	10-15	1940	1973
801	Penguin Part of set (see 802 & 803 Novelties)	2	10-15	1940	1973
817/1	Mallard	7½	75-80	1940	1969
817/2	Mallard	6¾	65-70	1940	1969
820	Two Geese	4	15-20	1940	1973
821	Goose (baby)	2¼	10-15	1940	1973
822	Goose (baby)	1¾	10-15	1940	1973
827/1	Goose	7½	60-65	1940	1955
827/2	Goose	6	55-60	1940	1955
827/3	Goose	5	50-55	1940	1955
849	Pheasant (in flight)	6	75-85	1940	1971
850	Pheasant (in flight)	5¾	75-85	1940	1971
862	Fan-Tail Pigeon	—	65-70	1940	1955
902	Mallard*	10	65-70	1940	1967
919/1	Duck	3¾	10-15	1941	1971
919/2	Duck	2⅝	5-10	1941	1971
919/3	Duck	2	5-10	1941	1971
925	Two American Blue Jays	4¾	55-60	1941	1973
926	Two Baltimore Orioles	4⅞	55-60	1941	1973
927	Cockatoo Cardinal	6	50-55	1941	1973
928	Tanager	—	45-50	1941	1973
929	Chickadee	5¾	45-50	1941	1967
930	Parakeet	6	45-50	1941	1973
980/1	Robin	3	10-15	1942	1973
980/2	Robin	3	9·50	1973	C
991/1	Chaffinch	2¾	10-15	1943	1973
991/2	Chaffinch	2¾	9·50	1973	C
992/1	Blue Tit	2½	10-15	1943	1946

*makes set of five with model No. 756

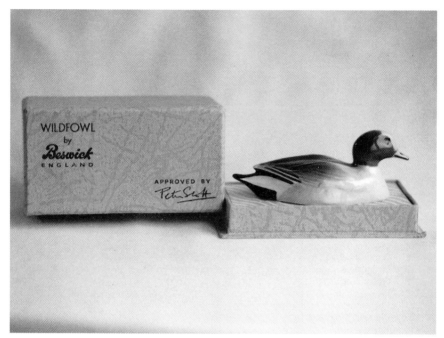

1526 *Widgeon and packing box*

1684-87 *Swans and Cygnets*

992/2	Blue Tit	2½	9·50	1946	C
993/1	Wren	2¼	10-15	1943	1973
993/2	Wren	2¼	9·50	1973	C
994	Sheldrake in flight	6	85-95	1943	1973
995	Sheldrake in flight	6½	85-95	1943	1970
1015	Two Penguins (courting)	5½	65-70	1945	1967
1018	Bald Eagle	7¼	45·00	1945	C
1022	Two Turtle Doves	7½	120-130	1945	1969
1041/1	Grey Wagtail	2½	10-15	1945	1973
1041/2	Grey Wagtail	2½	9·50	1973	C
1042/1	Bullfinch	2½	10-15	1945	1973
1042/2	Bullfinch	2½	9·50	1973	C
1046	Barn Owl	7¾	29.95	1946	C
1052	Barnacle Goose	6½	150-175	1946	1967
1159	Kookaburra	5¾	65-70	1949	1976
1178	Gouldian Finch (wings out)	4	65-70	1949	1967
1179	Gouldian Finch (wings in)	4	65-70	1949	1967
1180	Cockatoo (2 colourways)	8½	85-95	1949	1975
1212	Three Ducks pin tray	2¾	10-15	1951	1971
1216	Budgerigar	7	65-70	1951	1975
1217	Budgerigar	7	65-70	1951	1969
1218	Green Woodpecker	9	65-70	1951	1989
1219	Jay	6	85-95	1951	1971
1225	Pheasant	7¾	65-70	1951	1977
1226	Pheasant	6	50-60	1951	1977
1383	Pigeon (blue or red)	5½	45-50	1955	1989
1413	Bird (CM series)	3⅛	75-85	1956	1967
1415	Small Bird (CM series)	2¼	65-75	1956	1967
1416	Cock (CM series)	5¾	75-85	1956	1967
1420	Owl (CM series)	5¼	75-85	1956	1967
1462	Owl (CM series)	—	65-75	1956	1967
1467	Cock (CM series)	11¾	85-95	1956	1967
1471	Goose (CM series)	3¼	75-85	1957	1967
1482	Peacock (CM series)	3½	75-85	1957	1967
1503	Toucan	—	90-100	1957	1967
1518/1	Mallard Duck	1⅜	40-45	1958	1967
1518/2	Mallard Duck	1⅝	50-55	1958	1967
1518/3	Mallard Duck (re-modelled 1962)	1¾	60-65	1958	1967
1519/1	Mandarin Duck	1¼	40-45	1958	1967
1519/2	Mandarin Duck	1⅝	50-55	1958	1967
1519/3	Mandarin Duck	1⅞	60-65	1958	1967
1520/1	Pochard Duck	1	40-45	1958	1967
1520/2	Pochard Duck	1¼	50-55	1958	1967
1520/3	Pochard Duck	1½	60-65	1958	1967
1521	King Eider Duck	1¾	40-50	1958	1967
1522	Smew Duck	1¼	40-50	1958	1967
1523	Tufted Duck	1¼	40-50	1958	1967
1524	Goldeneye Duck	1⅝	40-50	1958	1967
1525	Goosander Duck	1¼	40-50	1958	1967
1526	Widgeon Duck	1¼	40-50	1958	1967
1527	Shelduck	1¾	40-50	1958	1967
1528	Shoveller	1⅛	35-40	1958	1967
1529	Teal Duck	1	35-40	1958	1967
1555	Peacock (head to side)	8	40-45	1958	1967

2059 *Gamecock*

2307 *Eagle on Rock and* **2063** *Pair of Grouse*

1556	Peacock (head to front) both flower holders	8	40-45	1958	1967
1614	Fantail Pigeon	5	100-120	1959	1969
1684	Swan	3	25-30	1960	1971
1685	Swan	2	25-30	1960	1971
1686	Cygnet	1	15-20	1960	1971
1687	Cygnet	1	15-20	1960	1971
1759	Pheasant	—	65-70	1961	1967
1774	Pheasant	$4\frac{3}{4}$	55-60	1961	1975
1818	Cockatoo (2 colourways)	$11\frac{1}{2}$	120-130	1962	1973
1892	Leghorn Cockerel	9	100-125	1963	1983
1899	Sussex Cockerel	7	125-150	1963	1971
1957	Turkey	$7\frac{1}{4}$	125-150	1964	1969
2026	Owl	$4\frac{5}{8}$	11·95	1965	C
2059	Gamecock	$9\frac{1}{2}$	125-150	1966	1973
2062	Golden Eagle	$9\frac{1}{2}$	80-90	1966	1989
2063	Grouse (pair)	$5\frac{1}{2}$	125-150	1966	1975
2064	Partridge (pair)	$5\frac{1}{2}$	125-150	1966	1975
2067	Turkey (miniature)	$2\frac{3}{8}$	45-50	1966	1969
2071	Owl	$5\frac{1}{8}$	40-45	1966	1967
2078	Pheasants (pair)	$6\frac{3}{4}$	125-150	1966	1975
2105/1	Greenfinch	3	10-15	1967	1973
2105/2	Greenfinch	3	9·50	1973	C
2106/1	Whitethroat	$2\frac{7}{8}$	10-15	1967	1973
2106/2	Whitethroat	$2\frac{7}{8}$	9·50	1973	C
2183	Baltimore Oriole	$3\frac{7}{8}$	65-70	1968	1973
2184	Cedar Wax-wing	$4\frac{5}{8}$	65-70	1968	1973
2187	American Robin	$4\frac{1}{8}$	65-70	1968	1973
2188	Blue Jay	$4\frac{3}{8}$	65-70	1968	1973
2189	Black Capped Chickadee	$4\frac{1}{2}$	65-70	1968	1973
2190	Evening Crosbeak	4	65-70	1968	1973
2191	Quail	$4\frac{7}{8}$	65-70	1968	1973
2199	Cockerel ash tray	8 long	20-25	1968	1971
2209	Pheasant ash tray	$12\frac{3}{4}$ long	25-30	1968	1971
2238	Owl	$6\frac{3}{4}$	30-35	1968	1971
2239	Bird	5	30-35	1968	1971
2240	Cock	6	30-35	1968	1971
2273	Goldfinch	3	9·50	1969	C
2274	Stonechat	3	9·50	1969	C
2305	Magpie	5	55-60	1970	1982
2307	Eagle on Rock	$3\frac{3}{4}$	35-40	1970	1975
2308	Song Thrush	$5\frac{3}{4}$	55-60	1970	1989
2315	Cuckoo	5	55-60	1970	1982
2316	Kestrel	$6\frac{3}{4}$	45-50	1970	1989
2357	Penguin	12	275-300	1971	1976
2359	Stork	$10\frac{1}{2}$	65-75	1971	1973
2371	Kingfisher	5	27·00	1971	C
2398	Penguin baby standing	$6\frac{7}{8}$	85-95	1971	1976
2399	Penguin chick	—	85-95	1972	1973
2413	Nuthatch	3	9·50	1972	C
2415	Gold Crest	$2\frac{5}{8}$	9·50	1972	C
2416	Lapwing	$5\frac{3}{8}$	55-60	1972	1982
2417	Jay	$5\frac{1}{8}$	55-60	1972	1982
2420	Lesser Spotted Woodpecker	$5\frac{1}{2}$	55-60	1972	1982
2434	Penguin baby sliding	8 long	85-95	1972	1976
2760	Pheasant	$10\frac{1}{2}$	150-160	1981	1990

3272	Tawny Owl	7·95	1991	C
3273	Barn Owl	7·95	1991	C
3274	Great Tit	9·95	1991	C
3275	Kingfisher	9·95	1991	C

C Current

Bird Wall Plaques (All models carry the Beswick mark)

Model No	Name of Model	Height inches	Value £	Design Date	Withdrawn By
596/0	Mallard	11¾	125-150 per set	1938	1971
596/1	Mallard	10	125-150 per set	1938	1973
596/2	Mallard	8¾	125-150 per set	1938	1973
596/3	Mallard	7	125-150 per set	1938	1973
596/4	Mallard	5¾	125-150 per set	1938	1971
658/1	Seagull	14	100-120 per set	1938	1967
658/2	Seagull	11¾	100-120 per set	1938	1967
658/3	Seagull	10⅛	100-120 per set	1938	1967
658/4	Seagull	8	100-120 per set	1938	1967
661/1	Pheasant	12	85-95 per set	1938	1971
661/2	Pheasant	10½	85-95 per set	1938	1971
661/3	Pheasant	8½	85-95 per set	1938	1971
705	Blue Tit (facing right)	4½	30-35	1939	1967
706	Blue Tit (facing left)	4½	30-35	1939	1967
707	Blue Tit (wings up)	4½	30-35	1939	1967
729/1	Kingfisher	7½	85-95 per set	1939	1971
729/2	Kingfisher	6	85-95 per set	1939	1971
729/3	Kingfisher	5	85-95 per set	1939	1971
731	Flamingo	15 long	200-250	1939	1955
*743	Kingfisher	6	45-50	1939	1955
757/1	Swallow	6	75-85 per set	1939	1973
757/2	Swallow	5	75-85 per set	1939	1973
757/3	Swallow	4	75-85 per set	1939	1973
922/1	Seagull	12	85-95 per set	1941	1971
922/2	Seagull	10½	85-95 per set	1941	1971
922/3	Seagull	9½	85-95 per set	1941	1971
1023/1	Humming Bird	5¾	150-175 per set	1945	1967
1023/2	Humming Bird	5	150-175 per set	1945	1967
1023/3	Humming Bird	4¾	150-175 per set	1945	1967
1188/1	Pink Legged Partridge	10½	150-175 per set	1950	1967
1188/2	Pink Legged Partridge	9	150-175 per set	1950	1967
1188/3	Pink Legged Partridge	7½	150-175 per set	1950	1967
1344/1	Green Woodpecker	7½	150-175 per set	1954	1967
1344/2	Green Woodpecker	6	150-175 per set	1954	1967
1344/3	Green Woodpecker	5	150-175 per set	1954	1967
1530/1	Teal	8¼	150-175 per set	1958	1967
1530/2	Teal	7¼	150-175 per set	1958	1967
1530/3	Teal	6¼	150-175 per set	1958	1967

*Pairs with 729/2 but flying in opposite direction

Butterfly Plaques (All models carry the Beswick mark)

A small number of delightful butterfly wall plaques were modelled by Albert Hallam, early in 1957. These are difficult to find, so it would seem that only a small number were produced. They are also easily damaged and therefore collectors must pay careful attention to condition.

Model No	Name of Model	Height inches	Value £	Design Date	Withdrawn By
1487	Purple Emperor (large)	—	175-200	1957	1967
1488	Red Admiral (large)	—	175-200	1957	1967
1989	Peacock (large)	—	175-200	1957	1967
1490	Clouded Yellow (medium)	5¼ x 3½	150-175	1957	1967
1491	Large Tortoiseshell (medium)	5¼ x 3½	150-175	1957	1967
1492	Swallow Tail (medium)	5¼ x 3½	150-175	1957	1967
1493	Small Copper (small)	3¾ x 2¼	125-150	1957	1967
1494	Purple Hairstreak (small)	3¾ x 2¼	125-150	1957	1967
1495	Small Heath (small)	3¾ x 2¼	125-150	1957	1967

*Top: **1489** Peacock Butterfly plaque; Bottom: **1490** Clouded Yellow Butterfly plaque*

Cats (All current cats produced since August 1989 carry a Royal Doulton backstamp)

The Beswick collection includes all types of cats from mischievous moggies to sleek pedigrees. As seven of the Beswick modellers have been commissioned to submit cat models over the years, the cat enthusiast can acquire an interesting and stylistically varied collection. A kitten wearing a bow featured in the Beswick catalogues at the turn of the century but no more cats appeared until 1945. Since then, felines have been consistently popular.

Miss Granoska's pair of Siamese kittens, for example, which was first introduced in 1953, is still being made today. Another long term favourite is the Fireside model, also a Siamese, which was introduced in 1967. Siamese and Persians tend to be the most popular of all the breeds, certainly they are the best represented at cat shows, and this is borne out by the current collection of pedigree models.

Beswick artists have also enjoyed putting cats in humorous situations curled up on a chimney pot or playing a musical instrument and these are featured in the comic animals section.

*1880 Persian Cat; **1886** Persian Kitten; **3139** Mouse teapot*

*L—R: **1897** Siamese Cat (in black colour variation); **1316** Persian kittens; **1885** Kitten*

Model No	Name of Model	Height inches	Value £	DA No	Design Date	Withdrawn By
1030	Cat	6¼	40-45		1945	1973
1031	Cat	4½	35-40		1945	1973
1296	Siamese Kittens	2¾	9·95	122	1953	C
1316	Persian Kittens	3½	30-35		1953	1973
1412	Cat (CM series)	9⅝	85-95		1956	1970
1417	Kitten (CM series)	5⅝	60-65		1956	1970
1435	Cat	5¼	60-65		1956	1967
1436	Kitten	3¼	5·50	123	1956	C
1437	Cat	—	60-65		1956	1967
1438	Cat	—	60-65		1956	1967
1474	Cat (CM series)	5¼	60-65		1957	1970
1541	Cat (large)	—	85-95		1958	1967
1542	Cat	—	60-65		1958	1967
1543	Cat	3	60-65		1958	1967
1558	Siamese lying	7¼	14·95	124	1958	C
1559	Siamese lying	7¼	14·95	125	1958	C
*1560	Cat	10¾	75-80		1958	1970
*1561	Cat	10¾	75-80		1958	1970
**1677	Cat climbing (part of set see 1678 Wild Animals)	7½	9·95		1960	C
1803	Cat singing (part of Bedtime Chorus set see Figures)	1½	25-30		1962	1971
1857	Kitten climbing	—	45-50		1962	1965
1867	Persian Cat sitting	8½	23-25	126	1963	C

* Available facing left or right and coloured white (zodiac signs) or black (plain)
**Still carries a Beswick backstamp

1876	Cat	$3\frac{1}{2}$	65-75		1963	1971
1877	Cat	$6\frac{1}{2}$	75-85		1963	1971
1880	Persian Cat	$5\frac{1}{4}$	65-75		1963	1971
1882	Siamese Cat	$9\frac{1}{2}$	25·00	127	1963	C
1883	Cat	$6\frac{1}{2}$	75-85		1963	1971
1885	Persian Kitten	$4\frac{3}{4}$	65-75		1963	1973
1886	Persian Kitten	4	8-9	128	1963	C
1887	Siamese Cat sitting	$4\frac{1}{8}$	8·25	129	1963	C
1897	Siamese Cat standing	$6\frac{1}{2}$	18·95	130	1963	C
1897	Cat (black)	$6\frac{1}{2}$	18·95	131	1987	C
1898	Persian Cat standing	5	13-19	132	1963	C
2139	Siamese Fireside Cat sitting	$13\frac{3}{4}$	49·95	83	1967	C
2301	Cat climbing (part of set see 2302 Wild Animals)	$4\frac{1}{2}$	30-35		1969	1971
2311	Siamese Cat	$1\frac{1}{2}$	25-30		1970	1973

C Current

*l—R: **1886** Persian Kitten; **1882** Siamese cat; **1876** Cat; **1030** Cat*

Connoisseur Series
(All current models carry a Royal Doulton backstamp)

The models in this series of animal and bird studies form a highly specialised branch of the potters art, with a long and distinguished tradition to follow.

The series falls into five distinct groups — Cattle, Horses, Dogs, Wildlife Animals and Birds — and most of these are available on a polished wood base with an inscribed metal plate giving a description of the model.

Each piece represents a completely natural study and captures all the grace, strength and bearing of the real animal or bird portrayed.

Every muscle, feather and feature is accurate and the finished models are a tribute to the skills and knowledge of the John Beswick Studio sculptors and artists.

The series was introduced in 1967 with a very detailed model of the racehorse 'Arkle' (2065) owned by Anne, Duchess of Westminster and trained by Mr T. Dreaper in Ireland. The horse was mounted on a hardwood base and was the forerunner of many more finely detailed models.

The success of this initial model prompted Beswick to widen the scope of the series and a number of models, already in production, were then added to the series, wood bases being used as appropriate.

Model No	Name of Model	Height inches	Value £	DA No	Design Date	Withdrawn By
998	Elephant	10¼	150-175		1943	1975
*1265	Arab Xayal Horse	7⅛	65-75		1952	1989
*1363	Hereford Bull	5⅜	90-100		1955	1975
*1564	Racehorse	12⅛	90-100		1959	1980
1702	Puma tawny	8½	90-100		1960	1989
*1734	Hunter dapple	12⅛	90-100		1961	1983
1770	Indian Elephant	12	150-175		1961	1982
*1771	Arab dapple	8⅛	65-75		1961	1989
*1772	Thoroughbred Horse	8⅞	65-75		1961	1989
*1933	Beagle	5⅞	65-75		1964	1989
*2045	Basset Hound	5⅞	65-75		1965	1989
2062	Golden Eagle	9½	80-90		1966	1989
*2065	'Arkle' racehorse	11⅞	139·00	15	1966	C
*2084	'Arkle' Pat Taaffe up	12⅝	165-185		1966	1980
*2210	Highwayman on horse	13⅞	300-350		1968	1975
*2269	Arab Stallion with authentic saddle	9½	200-250		1969	1973
*2275	Bedouin Arab on horse	11½	300-350		1969	1973
2309	Shire Horse	10 ¾	55-65		1970	1982
*2340	'Cardigan Bay' racehorse	9¼	300-350		1970	1976
*2345	'Nijinsky' racehorse	11⅛	139·00	16	1970	C
*2352	'Nijinsky' Lester Piggott up	12⅝	175-195		1971	1982
*2422	'Mill Reef' racehorse	9	100-120		1972	1989
*2431	Mountie Stallion	10	175-200		1972	1975
*2463	Charolais Bull	5⅜	90-100		1975	1979

2275 *Bedouin Arab on Horse*

2269 *Arab stallion with authentic saddle*

*2466/ 2536	'Black Beauty' & foal	7¾	69·95	17	1973	C
*2510	'Red Rum' racehorse	12½	139·00	18	1974	C
*2511	'Red Rum' Brian Fletcher up	13	165-185		1974	1983
*2535	'Psalm' Ann Moore up	12¾	145-165		1975	1982
*2540	'Psalm' racehorse	11½	100-120		1975	1982
*2541	Welsh Mountain Pony	9	120-140		1975	1989
*2542	Hereford Bull	7½	119·00	19	1975	C
2554	Lion on rock	8¼	70-80		1975	1983
*2558	'Grundy' racehorse	11¼	139·00	20	1976	C
*2562	Lifeguard on horse	14½	325·00	22	1976	C
*2574	Polled Hereford Bull	7½	119·00	21	1976	C
*2580	Friesian Bull	7⅜	119·00	23	1976	C
*2581	Collie	8¼	69·95	24	1976	C
*2582	Blues and Royals — mounted	14½	325·00	25	1987	C
*2587	Alsatian	8⅞	69·95	26	1977	C
*2600	Charolais Bull	7½	119·00	27	1977	C
*2605	Morgan Horse	11½	119·00	28	1977	C
2607	Friesian Cow	7½	119·00	29	1977	C
*2607/ 2690	Friesian Cow & calf	7½	139·00	30	1980	C
*2608	'The Minstrel' racehorse	13½	139·00	31	1978	C
**2629	Stag	13½	149·00	32	1978	C
*2648/ 2652	Charolais Cow & calf	7¼	139·00	33	1979	C
*2667/ 2669	Hereford Cow & calf	7	139·00	34	1980	C
2671	'Moonlight' horse	11¼	95·00	35	1980	C
2671	'Sunburst' horse	11¼	95·00	36	1986	C
**2671	'Nightshade' horse	11¼	149·00	35	1986	C
*2674	'Troy' racehorse	11¾	139·00	37	1980	C
**2725	Cheetah on rock	6½	149·00	39	1981	C
**2760	Pheasant	10½	235·00	38	1981	C

* Mounted on polished wooden base.
**On wooden base from 1990
NOTES:
2629	Stag is now called Majestic Stag
2671	Nightshade is now called Champion
2725	Cheetah on Rock is now called The Watering Hole
2760	Pheasant is now called Open Ground (all with re-modelled bases)

Dogs (All current models carry a Beswick backstamp unless allocated a "DA' number. These are backstamped Royal Doulton)

There is no doubt that the dog is man's best friend whether it be as a hunter, guard or, most commonly, a companion. Always ready for a game or a walk and only asking for food and a bed, he amply repays all the love and attention given to him.

As early as 1898, Beswick had introduced models of dogs as mantlepiece ornaments. These Old English Dogs are still made today and are very popular. Since 1934, over a hundred dogs have appeared in the pattern books from frisky mongrels to pedigree show dogs. According to the Kennel Club there are approximately seventy different species of dog and about two hundred varieties in all, so there is still plenty of scope for the Beswick modellers.

A problem with selecting a champion dog is that breeders have different conceptions of the true characteristics of a winner or top dog, thus it is a challenge to achieve a model which is approved by all. The very best of the championship winners are singled out to pose for Beswick, with a team of experts advising on the final product. Crufts judges, for example, assess the clay reproduction and suggest improvements until satisfied that the 'conformation' is exact. Few potteries can compete against such high standards.

Model No	Name of Model	Height inches	Value £	DA No	Design Date	Withdrawn By
3	Mantlepiece Dog	10	50-60		1933	1955
4	Mantlepiece Dog	9	30-35		1933	1955
5	Mantlepiece Dog	7½	25-30		1933	1955
6	Mantlepiece Dog	5½	15-20		1933	1955
88	Dog ash tray	3¼	15-20		1934	1965
171	Dog begging	4¾	45-50		1934	1954
286	Dog	6	20-25		1934	1967
301	Sealyham plaque	7½	45-55		1935	1940
302	Sealyham	5¾	25-30		1935	1967
307	Dog plaque	—	45-55		1935	1940
*308	Dog sitting	6	25-30		1935	1967
361	Dachshund re-modelled 1956	5½	25-30		1936	1982
373	Dog plaque	7	45-55		1936	1940
453	Old English Sheep Dog sitting	8½	70-80		1936	1973
454	Dog sitting	4¼	25-30		1936	1969
668	Dog plaque	10 x 11	100-120		1938	1960
752	Scottie (as model 87)	—	25-30		1939	1954
753	Sealyham	—	25-30		1939	1954
810	Bulldog ash tray (sailors hat)	4	35-40		1940	1970
869	Five dogs ash tray	2	15-20		1940	1967
916	Three dogs ash tray	2	10-15		1941	1967
917	Three dogs (as 916 ash tray)	2	10-15		1941	1965
**941	Foxhound (see 2263)	2⅞	10-15		1941	1969

*Also found as a money box   **Re-modelled 1969 with thinner tail and legs

1998 Pug; *1814* Collie; *1460* and *1461* Dachshunds; *1762* Alsatian; *1852* Boxer

1876/1 Whippet (1st version)

L—R: **2299** *Doberman Pinscher;* **3260** *and* **3055** *Rottweilers*

2023 *Jack Russell;* **971** *Sealyham*

**942	Foxhound (see 2265)	2¾	10-15		1941	1969
**943	Foxhound (see 2264)	2⅞	10-15		1941	1969
**944	Foxhound (see 2262)	2½	10-15		1941	1969
961	Dalmation 'Arnoldene'	5¾	23·00		1941	C
962	Airedale 'Cast Iron Monarch'	5½	20-25		1941	1989
963	Wire-haired Fox Terrier 'Talavera Romulus'	5¾	25-30		1941	1983
964	Smooth Fox Terrier 'Endon Black Rod'	5½	75-85		1941	1973
965	Bulldog 'Basford British Mascot'	5½	30-35		1941	1989
966	Irish Setter 'Sugar of Wendover'	5¾	20-25		1941	1989
967	Cocker Spaniel 'Horseshoe Primular'	5¾	23·00		1941	C
968	Great Dane 'Ruler of Oubourgh'	7	23·00		1941	C
969	Alsatian 'Ulrica of Brittas'	5¾	23·00		1942	C
970	Bull Terrier 'Romany Rhinestone'	5⅝	23·00		1942	C
971	Sealyham 'Forestedge Foxglove'	4	75-85		1942	1967
972	Greyhound 'Jovial Rodger'	6	30-35		1942	1989
973	English Setter 'Bayledone Baronet'	5½	20-25		1942	1989
1055	Cairn Terrier with ball	4	30-35		1946	1969
1057	Spaniel running	3¾	30-35		1946	1967
1059	Pekinese begging	4¼	30-35		1946	1967
1060	Red Setter lying down	3	30-35		1946	1973
1061	Dog lying down	2	30-35		1946	1973
1062	Terrier	4	30-35		1946	1973
1202	Boxer 'Brindle'	5½	30-35		1950	1988
1220	English Setter (large)	8	60-65		1951	1973
1239	Dog begging (from model 1086)	2½	40-45		1952	1967
1240	Dog sitting (from model 1096)	2⅛	40-45		1952	1967
1241	Dog howling from model 909	1¼	30-35		1952	1967
1242	Dog barking (from model 906)	1⅛	30-35		1952	1967
1294	Poodle 'Ebonit Av Barbette''	—	85-95		1953	1967
1299	Corgi 'Black Prince'	5⅝	23·00		1953	C
ø1378/1	Old English Dog	13¼	75-80		1955	1976
ø1378/2	Old English Dog	11½	65-70		1955	1972
ø1378/3	Old English Dog	10	45·00†	89/90	1955	C
ø1378/4	Old English Dog	9	29·95†	91/92	1955	C
ø1378/5	Old English Dog	7½	23·00†	93/94	1955	C
ø1378/6	Old English Dog	5½	14·95†	95/96	1955	C
ø1378/7	Old English Dog	3½	8·95†	97/98	1955	C
1386	Poodle	3½	10-15		1955	1989
1460	Dachshund	2¾	9·50		1956	C
1461	Dachshund begging	4	15-20		1957	1980

**Re-modelled 1969 with thinner tail and legs øAvailable in left and right hand versions
†Priced per pair

1463	Bulldog (CM series)	—	60-65		1956	1970
1469	Dachshund (CM series)	—	60-65		1957	1970
1472	Poodle (CM series)	$5\frac{3}{4}$	60-65		1957	1970
1548	Labrador Dog 'Solomon of Wendover'	$5\frac{1}{2}$	23·00		1958	C
1731	Bulldog 'Bosun'	$2\frac{1}{2}$	9·50		1960	C
1736	Corgi	$2\frac{3}{4}$	9·50		1961	C
1753	Bull Terrier	$3\frac{1}{2}$	55-60		1961	1971
1754	Cocker Spaniel	3	9·50		1961	C
1762	Alsatian	$3\frac{1}{4}$	30-35		1961	1965
1763	Dalmatian	$3\frac{1}{2}$	9·50		1961	C
1786/1	Whippet (tail curved down between legs)	$4\frac{1}{2}$	35-40		1961	1983
1786/2	Whippet (tail attached to back leg)	$4\frac{1}{2}$	30-35		1983	1989
1791	Collie 'Lochinvar of Ladypark'	$5\frac{3}{4}$	23·00		1961	C
1792	Sheep Dog	$5\frac{1}{2}$	23·00		1961	C
1814	Collie	$3\frac{1}{4}$	25-30		1962	1975
1824	Small dog singing (part of Bedtime Chorus Set — see Figures)	$1\frac{3}{8}$	30-35		1962	1971
1852	Boxer	3	35-40		1962	1975
1854	Sheep Dog	3	9·50		1962	C
1855	Retriever	$3\frac{1}{4}$	25-30		1962	1975
1932	Dachshund ash tray	5	25-30		1962	1969
1933	Beagle	5	30-35		1964	1989
1939	Beagle	3	9·50		1964	C
1944	Yorkshire Terrier	$3\frac{1}{2}$	35-40		1964	1975
1956	Labrador	$3\frac{1}{4}$	9·50		1964	C
1982	Staffordshire Bull Terrier 'Bandits Brintiga'	$4\frac{3}{4}$	85-95		1964	1969
1997	Pug 'Cutmil Cupie'	$4\frac{1}{2}$	55-60		1965	1982
1998	Pug	$2\frac{1}{2}$	20-25		1966	1989
2023	Jack Russell	5	23·00		1965	C
2037	Scottie	$4\frac{1}{2}$	20-25		1965	1989
2038	West Highland Terrier	$4\frac{3}{4}$	23·00		1965	C
2045	Basset Hound	5	23·00		1965	C
2107A	King Charles Spaniel 'Blenheim' brown/white	$5\frac{1}{4}$	23·00		1967	C
2107B	King Charles Spaniel 'Josephine of Blagreaves' Black, Brown & White	$5\frac{1}{2}$	23·00		1967	C
2108	Poodle 'Ivanola Gold Digger'	$5\frac{3}{4}$	75-85		1967	1971
2109	Jack Russel Terrier	$2\frac{5}{8}$	9·50		1967	C
2112	Cairn Terrier	$2\frac{3}{4}$	9·50		1967	C
2221	St Bernard 'Corna Garth Stroller'	$5\frac{3}{4}$	30-35		1968	1988
2232	Old English Sheep Dog	$11\frac{1}{2}$	75·00	84	1968	C
2262	Foxhound (see 944)	$2\frac{1}{2}$	7·50		1969	C
2263	Foxhound (see 941)	$2\frac{7}{8}$	7·50		1969	C
2264	Foxhound (see 943)	$2\frac{7}{8}$	7·50		1969	C
2265	Foxhound (see 942)	$2\frac{3}{4}$	7·50		1969	C
2271	Dalmatian sitting	$13\frac{3}{4}$	75·00	85	1969	C
2285	Afghan Hound 'Hajubah of Davlen'	$5\frac{1}{2}$	23·00		1969	C
2286	Dachshund	$10\frac{1}{2}$	45-50		1969	1982

2287	Golden Retriever 'Cabus Cadet'	$5\frac{3}{4}$	23·00		1969	C
2299	Doberman Pinscher 'Annastock Lance'	$5\frac{3}{4}$	23·00		1970	C
2300	Beagle sitting	$12\frac{3}{4}$	90-100		1969	1982
2314	Labrador	$13\frac{1}{2}$	75·00	86	1970	C
2339	Poodle	$5\frac{3}{4}$	30-35		1970	1982
2377	Yorkshire Terrier	$10\frac{1}{4}$	49·95	87	1971	C
2410	Alsatian	14	75·00	88	1972	C
2448	Lakeland Terrier	$3\frac{1}{4}$	9·50		1973	C
2454	Chihuahua	$2\frac{7}{8}$	9·50		1973	C
2929	Collie Head — on wood mount	$5\frac{3}{4}$	20-25		1986	1988
2932	Alsatian Head — on wood mount	$5\frac{3}{4}$	20-25		1986	1988
*2946	Meal Time	$3\frac{1}{2}$	15-20		1987	1988
*2947	Gnawing	$4\frac{1}{4}$	15-20		1987	1988
*2948	Play Time	$3\frac{3}{4}$	15-20		1987	1988
*2949	Juggling	3	15-20		1987	1988
*2950	Nap Time	$4\frac{1}{2}$	15-20		1987	1988
*2951	Caught It	$2\frac{3}{4}$	15-20		1987	1988
**2980	Cocker Spaniel on base	$8\frac{1}{4}$	49·95	108	1986	C
**2982	Pekinese	$5\frac{1}{2}$	19·95	113	1986	C
**2984	Norfolk Terrier	4	19·95	114	1986	C
**2985	Poodle on cushion	5	24·95	115	1986	C
**2986	English Setter on base	$8\frac{1}{2}$	49·95	109	1986	C
**3011	English Pointer on base	$7'\frac{3}{4}$	49·95	110	1986	C
**3013	Dachshund	$4\frac{1}{2}$	19·95	116	1986	C
**3055	Rottweiler	$5\frac{1}{2}$	25·00	99	1988	C
3058	Old English Sheepdog	$5\frac{1}{2}$	25·00	100	1988	C
3060	Staffordshire Bull Terrier	4	25·00	101	1988	C
3062	Labrador on base	$6\frac{1}{2}$	49·95	111	1988	C
3066	Retriever on base	$7\frac{1}{2}$	49·95	112	1988	C
3070	Afghan Hound	$5\frac{1}{2}$	25·00	102	1988	C
3073	Alsatian	$5\frac{3}{4}$	25·00	103	1988	C
3080	Shetland Sheepdog	5	19·95	117	1988	C
3081	Boxer	$5\frac{1}{2}$	25·00	104	1988	C
3082	Cairn Terrier	$4\frac{1}{2}$	19·95	118	1988	C
3083	Yorkshire Terrier	5	19·95	119	1988	C
3121	Doberman	$5\frac{1}{4}$	25·00	105	1989	C
3129	Rough Collie	$5\frac{1}{2}$	25·00	106	1989	C
3135	Springer Spaniel	5	25·00	107	1989	C
3149	West Highland Terrier white	5	19·95	120	1989	C
3155	Cavalier King Charles Spaniel	5	27·00	121	1989	C
3258	Alsatian	$3\frac{1}{4}$	9·95		1991	C
3260	Rottweiler	$3\frac{1}{4}$	9·95		1991	C
3262	Yorkshire Terrier	$3\frac{1}{4}$	9·95		1991	C
3270	Retriever	3	9·95		1991	C

*These six dogs were taken out of Doulton Character Dog HN range (Nos 1158, 1159, 2654, 1103, 1099 and 1097) and given Beswick numbers.
**Can also be found with the Beswick mark

Farm Animals

(All current farm animals carry the Beswick backstamp)

In order to maintain their reputation for realistic images of animals, authentic in every detail, Beswick designers have literally been 'down on the farm' for inspiration. Modellers have spent days in the field getting to know the subjects of their study in order to produce an accurate model which is a faithful representation of a champion breed. Many of the models actually carry the name of the award winning animal which inspired the artists. This is particularly true of the cattle and pigs which were modelled by Arthur Gredington. Introduced from 1952 onwards these are still very popular today, particularly among farming communities.

In recent years the champion breeds have been modelled by Graham Tongue and he recalls that the Charolais Bull which posed for his Connoisseur model in 1973 was the largest he had ever seen.

The recent pedigree bulls contrast dramatically with Beswick's first farm animal: a delightful lamb in playful mood modelled by Miss Greaves (323). This light-hearted approach can also be traced throughout the history of Beswick animals and has been revived recently in the Farmyard Humour collection which includes a snoozing piglet on the back of the mother pig (2746) and a modern version of the traditional Staffordshire cow-creamer, Daisy the Cow (2792) now withdrawn. These can be found in the 'Comical Animals and Birds' section.

1746 Belted Galloway

Model No	Name of Model	Height inches	Value £	Design Date	Withdrawn By
323	Lamb on base	—	70-75	1934	1954
369	Donkey on base	8	70-75	1936	1954
398	Goat	$4\frac{1}{2}$	25-30	1936	1954
832	Pig	$3\frac{3}{4}$	25-30	1940	1971
833	Piglet	$1\frac{3}{4}$	15-20	1940	1971
834	Piglet	$1\frac{1}{2}$	15-20	1940	1971
854	Hereford Calf	$4\frac{3}{4}$	50-55	1940	1973
897	Donkey Foal	$5\frac{3}{4}$	50-60	1941	1962
899	Cow	—	75-85	1941	1954
901	Hereford Calf	4	35-40	1940	1973
935	Sheep	$3\frac{1}{2}$	20-25	1941	1971
936	Lamb	$3\frac{1}{4}$	15-20	1941	1971
937	Lamb	2	10-15	1941	1971
938	Lamb	2	10-15	1941	1971
948	Hereford Cow	5	100-120	1941	1957
949	Hereford Bull	$5\frac{1}{2}$	100-120	1941	1957
950	Donkey Foal	$5\frac{3}{4}$	55-60	1941	1962
1035	Goat	$5\frac{1}{2}$	65-75	1945	1971
1036	Kid	$2\frac{1}{2}$	35-40	1945	1971
1248	Guernsey Cow	$4\frac{1}{4}$	45-50	1952	1990
1249	Jersey Calf	$2\frac{3}{4}$	9.95	1954	C
1249	Friesian Calf	$2\frac{3}{4}$	9.95	1954	C
1249	Ayrshire Calf	$2\frac{3}{4}$	15-20	1954	1990
1249	Guernsey Calf	$2\frac{3}{4}$	15-20	1952	1990
1345	Jersey Cow 'Newton Tinkle'	$4\frac{1}{4}$	25.00	1954	C
1350	Ayrshire Cow 'Ickham Bessie'	5	45-50	1954	1990
1360	Hereford Cow	$4\frac{1}{4}$	25.00	1954	C
1362	Friesian Cow 'Claybury Leegwater'	$4\frac{1}{2}$	25.00	1954	C
1363	Hereford Bull	$4\frac{1}{2}$	25.00	1955	C
1364	Donkey	$4\frac{1}{2}$	12.95	1955	C
1406	Dairy Shorthorn Calf	3	35-40	1957	1973
1406	Hereford Calf	3	30-35	1956	1975
1406	Aberdeen Angus Calf	3	30-35	1958	1975
1410	Cow (CM series)	$7\frac{1}{8}$	75-85	1956	1970
1422	Jersey Bull 'Dunsley Coy Boy'	$4\frac{1}{2}$	25.00	1956	C
1439	Friesian Bull 'Coddington Hilt Bar'	$4\frac{3}{4}$	29.95	1956	C
1451	Guernsey Bull 'Sabrina's Sir Richmond 14th'	$4\frac{3}{4}$	45-50	1956	1990
1452	White Sow 'Champion Wallqueen 40th'	$2\frac{3}{4}$	12.95	1956	C
1453	White Boar 'Wall Champion Boy 53rd'	$2\frac{3}{4}$	12.95	1956	C
1454	Ayrshire Bull 'Whitehill Mandate'	$5\frac{1}{4}$	45-50	1956	1990
1473	Pig (CM series)	$2\frac{1}{2}$	60-65	1957	1970
1504	Dairy Shorthorn Bull 'Gwersylt Lord Oxford 74th'	5	150-175	1957	1973
1510	Dairy Shorthorn Cow 'Eaton Wild Eyes 91st'	$4\frac{3}{4}$	150-175	1957	1973
1511	Sow 'Merrywood Silver Wings 56th' Saddleback	$2\frac{3}{4}$	125-150	1957	1969

1512	Boar 'Far Acre Viscount 3rd' Saddleback	2¾	125-150	1957	1969
1562	Aberdeen Angus Bull	4½	35-40	1958	1990
1563	Aberdeen Angus Cow	4¼	30-35	1959	1990
1740	Highland Cow	5½	35-40	1961	1990
1746	Galloway Bull 'Silver Dunn'	4½	175-200	1961	1969
1765	Black Faced Sheep	3¼	8.95	1961	C
1827	Highland Calf	3	15-20	1962	1990
1827	Hereford Calf	3	9.95	1985	C
1827	Aberdeen Angus Calf	3	15-20	1985	1990
1827	Charolais Calf	3	9.95	1985	C
1828	Black Faced Lamb	2⅜	4.95	1962	C
1917	Merino Ram	4½	125-150	1963	1967
2008	Highland Bull	5	40-45	1965	1990
2110	Donkey Foal	4⅜	8.95	1967	C
2267	Donkey	5½	14.95	1969	C
2463	Charolais Bull (small)	5	49.95	1975	C
2549	Polled Hereford Bull	5	49.95	1975	C
3071	Black Faced Ram	3½	12.95	1988	C
3075	Charolais Cow	4⅞	25.00	1988	C

Model numbers 1362, 1439 and 2690 were produced in a limited special colourway for members of the Beswick Collectors Circle only, in June 1992

Fish (All models carry the Beswick mark)

The sport of many is to sit in quiet solitude on the bank of an equally quiet river and hope that one's knowledge and skill will land a good catch. Any one of the excellent range of fish portrayed by Beswick would be an appropriate addition to the angler's collection.

Fish studies would appear to have been a new departure for Beswick, although an old catalogue contains an illustration of a dolphin jug.

All the models are supported on a base, some balanced on their tail whilst others lie horizontally. Often the fins and tail are vulnerable to damage and it is therefore difficult to find perfect examples.

As with all Beswick animal studies, a team of experts visited Beswick to verify the accuracy of each fish model. Not only were they concerned to check the size and proportions of the fish, but as Colin Melbourne remembers, the number of scales were actually counted!

Model No	Name of Model	Height inches	Value £	Design Date	Withdrawn By
1032	Trout	6¼	45-50	1945	1975
1047	Angel Fish	7¼	85-95	1946	1969
1232	Oceanic Bonito	7¼	85-95	1952	1969
1233	Atlantic Salmon	6½	85-95	1952	1969
1235	Barracuda	4¾	85-95	1952	1969
1243	Marlin	5½	85-95	1952	1969
1246	Golden Trout	6	85-95	1952	1969
1266	Large Mouthed Black Bass	5	85-95	1952	1969
1390	Trout (small)	4	35-40	1955	1975
1485	Black Bass	6	85-95	1957	1969

1599	Trout ash bowl	5	50-55	1959	1969
1874	Roach	4 ¼	85-95	1963	1969
1875	Perch	4 ¼	85-95	1963	1969
2066	Salmon	8	65-70	1966	1975
2087	Trout	6	50-55	1966	1975
2254	Fish	4 ⅝	50-55	1968	1969

Horses, Foals and Ponies

(All current items in this section produced since August 1989, carry a Royal Doulton backstamp)

This is the subject for which Beswick is best known and it is the largest section of all with over one hundred and fifty recorded models, fourteen being continuously in production for over thirty-five years.

The first horse (701), modelled by Arthur Gredington in 1939, was based on Bois Russell the winner of the 1938 Derby. It was innovatory as it introduced the concept of modelling from champions and named breeds. The **Pottery Gazette and Glass Trade Review** was quick to praise and appreciate John Beswick's new style. In April 1942 it wrote: ". . . among Beswick's wares were a host of splendidly modelled and lifelike animal subjects including some particularly fine horses and foals — both hunters and shires, this being a type of potting for which the firm has established a big reputation . . ."

Since Bois Russell, many famous racehorses have been immortalised by Beswick; Arkle, Grundy, Red Rum, Troy, Nijinski and Cardigan Bay being just some of the well known names among them. Until 1983 collectors could opt to have the horses ridden by equally famous jockeys such as Lester Pigott on Nijinski.

It has always been something of a gamble for the Beswick modellers to choose a horse which will continue to be as successful in the future as it has been in the past. The horse's owner is contacted and, once permission for the model is obtained, the modeller and design manager arrange a visit to study the animal. During the visit they meet and talk to all who are connected with the horse — the owner, the trainer and the grooms so that its personality can be fully understood. The horse is studied from all angles, particularly when it is at its most relaxed, paying particular attention to the pose, facial expressions, marks and, above all, its character. Sketches are made and photographs are taken to check that markings, colours and other details are accurate. Although all horses have a similar bone and muscle structure the expression and character of each is different and it is this which the modeller wishes to portray in clay. Back in the studio, the modeller starts working with the clay to put this into effect. The bone measurements and pose are positioned first and over this the rib cage and muscle structure are built up with sinews, veins, hair and mane following. In this way the physical appearance as well as the character and spirit of each horse is captured.

Throughout his work the sculptor has had to bear in mind the size of the finished model, the various methods of production, the type of decoration and the eventual price. The size is of particular importance since shrinkage of one twelfth occurs during firing. Consultations between the modeller and designer are frequent. The completed model is checked against the photographs and then the owner is invited to the factory to comment on its fidelity. One or two minor alterations are usually made as a result, and the finished, fully approved model then passes to the mould maker.

An early series of horses portrayed Mountain and Moorland ponies. In producing these, Beswick worked closely with R. S. Summerhays, a past President of the National Pony Society, who approved each model for accuracy of shape and colour. He also wrote an introduction with comments on each breed of pony for the accompanying sales brochure of the period.

Not all of Beswick's horses are based on named animals, but all must have the correct proportions and anatomical structure to maintain Beswick's high standards. Once these considerations are fulfilled, endless variations are possible.

Since 1981 Graham Tongue has romanticised the character of the horse in the 'Spirit' collection, with evocative names such as 'Spirit of Fire', 'Spirit of Freedom' and 'Spirit of Earth', the latter portraying a massive working horse. Clydesdales, Shires and Percherons have all featured in the collection over the years, some complete with leather harness. Originally the racehorse (1564) was also available with a detachable leather saddle. The first model to actually include a rider was the Huntsman (868), which is still current. Since then a Cowboy, an Indian, a Bedouin Arab, a Canadian Mountie, a Lifeguard and a Guardsman have all appeared on horseback. The Guardsman was modelled at Kensington Barracks and it took over two hours to model the details of his uniform alone. Equally faithful in every detail are the portraits of Her Majesty, Queen Elizabeth II on Imperial, and his Royal Highness, the Duke of Edinburgh on Alamein.

Model No	Name of Model	Height inches	Value £	DA No	Design Date	Withdrawn By
686	Horse's Head through a horseshoe looking left Plaque	7¼ x 6	75-85		1939	1967
687	Horse's Head through a horseshoe looking right Plaque	7¼ x 6	75-85		1939	1967
**701	'Bois Russell' Derby Winner 1938	8	21·00	42	1939	C
728	Foal	5	20-25		1939	1971
763	Foal (re-modelled 1956)	3¼	15-20		1939	1976
766	Foal on base	—	75-85		1939	1954
806	Horse's Head Plaque (as 686 with raised back)	7¼ x 6	75-85		1939	1954
807	Horse's Head Plaque (as 687 with raised back)	7¼ x 6	75-85		1939	1967
**815	Foal	3¼	7·50	74	1940	C

**Higher price for matt finish

818	Shire with or without harness	8½	21·00	43	1940	C
818	Black Shire special colourway for Beswick Collectors Circle only	8½	50-60		1990 only	
836	Foal (re-modelled 1958)	5	20-25		1940	1982
855	Horse	6	21·00	44	1940	C
*868	Huntsman on rearing horse on base (re-modelled 1952)	10	85·00		1940	C
**915	Foal lying	3¼	9·50	75	1941	C
939	Girl on horse jumping fence on base (horse as model 982)	9¾	125-150		1941	1962
**946	Foal	3¼	9·50	76	1941	C
**947	Foal	4½	10·95	77	1941	C
951	Foal (Shire)	6¼	20-25		1941	1971
953	Mare & Foal (on base)	7¾	75-85		1941	1983
975	Trotting Horse (Shire)	8¾	29·95	45	1942	C
**976	Mare	6¾	21·00	46	1942	C
982	Side saddle lady on horse jumping fence on base. (Horse as model 939)	10	125-150		1942	1967
996	Foal	3¼	10-15		1943	1976
**997	Foal	3¼	7·50	78	1943	C
1014	Prancing Horse on base	10¼	60-65		1945	1990
1033	Shetland Pony	5¾	17·95	47	1945	C
**1034	Shetland Foal	3¾	9·50	79	1945	C
1037	Horse & Jockey	8½	175-200		1945	1976
1050	Shire Horse grazing	5½	55-60		1946	1971
1053	Foal (Shire)	5	20-25		1946	1982
1084	Foal	4½	20-25		1947	1982
1085	Foal	3½	20-25		1947	1971
1145	15th Century Knight in armour, mounted on horse	10¾	850-900		1949	1969
**1182	Horse	8¾	25·00	48	1950	C
1197	Pony head up	5½	25-30		1950	1972
**1261	Palomino	6¾	21·00	49	1952	C
1265	Arab Xayal	6¼	21·00	50	1952	C
1359	'Hasse Dainty' Suffolk Punch	8	100-125		1954	1971
1361	Hackney Horse	7¾	50-55		1954	1982
1373/1	Pinto Horse (tail attached to leg)	6½	55-60		1955	1982
1373/2	Pinto Horse (tail hanging loose)	6½	40-45		1982	1990
1374	Galloping Palomino horse on base	7½	100-125		1955	1975
1375	Canadian Mountie	8¼	225-250		1955	1976
1377	Mounted Cowboy	8¾	300-350		1955	1969
1382	Hunter Horse Head	4 x 4	35-40		1955	1969
1384	Palomino Horse Head	4 x 4	35-40		1955	1969
1385	Arab Horse Head	4 x 4	35-40		1955	1969
1391	Mounted Indian	8½	175-200		1955	1990
**1407	Foal	4½	9·50	80	1956	C

*Still carries a Beswick backstamp   **Higher price for matt finish

1411	Horse (C.M. series)	8¾	75-85		1956	1971
1480	Pony (as 1500)	4	65-75		1957	1966
1483	Pony (as 1499)	5	65-75		1957	1966
1484	Hunter Horse (as 1501)	6¾	45-50		1957	1982
1499	Girl on Pony	5½	110-130		1957	1976
1500	Boy on Pony	5½	120-140		1957	1976
*1501	Huntsman	8¼	85·00		1957	C
1505	Huntsman (as 868) Plaque	10	100-125		1957	1962
1513	Lady on horse 'taking off' Plaque	9 x 4¼	100-125		1957	1962
1514	Man on horse 'landing' Plaque	8¾ x 7¾	100-125		1957	1962
1515	Lady on horse 'going over' Plaque	8 x 5½	100-125		1957	1962
1516	Appaloosa	5¼	150-175		1957	1966
1546	H.M. Queen Elizabeth II on 'Imperial'	10½	175-200		1958	1980
1549	Horse	7½	21·00	51	1958	C
1557	'Imperial' (modified from 1546)	8¼	55-60		1958	1982
1564	Racehorse with or without Saddle	11¼	85-95		1959	1980
1588	H.R.H. Duke of Edinburgh on 'Alamein'	10½	175-200		1958	1980
1624	Life Guard on horseback	9½	225-250		1959	1977
1641	Connemara Pony 'Terese of Leam'	7	60-65		1959	1983
1642	Dartmoor Pony 'Jentyl'	6¼	50-55		1959	1983
1643	Welsh Mountain Pony 'Coed Coch Madog'	6¼	40-45		1959	1989
1644	Highland Pony 'Mackinonneach'	7¼	40-45		1959	1989
1645	Exmoor Pony 'Heatherman'	6½	50-55		1959	1984
1646	New Forest Pony 'Jonathan 3rd'	7	50-55		1960	1983
1647	Fell Pony 'Dene Dauntless'	6¾	50-55		1960	1982
1648	Shetland Pony 'Eschon Chan Ronay'	4¾	40-45		1960	1989
1671	Dales Pony 'Maisie'	6½	50-55		1960	1982
*1730	Huntswoman	8¼	85·00		1960	C
1734	Hunter Horse	11¼	85-95		1961	1983
**1771	Arab Horse	7½	21·00	52	1961	C
1772	Thoroughbred Horse	8	21·00	53	1961	C
1772A	Appaloosa	8	49·95	68	1961	C
1793	Welsh Cob	7½	60-65		1962	1982
1811	Bay Mare & Foal on base	6	85-95		1962	1973
1812	Mare	5¾	25-30		1962	1990
**1813	Foal	4½	9·50	81	1962	C
**1816	Foal	3⅜	7·50	82	1962	C
1817	Foal	3¼	15-20		1962	1975
1862	Horse & Jockey	8	150-175		1963	1982
1918	Pony ash tray (model 1643)	11 x 8	50-55		1963	1972
**1991	Mare	5½	13·95	55	1964	C
**1992	Stallion	5½	13·95	56	1964	C

*Still carries a Beswick backstamp   **Higher price for matt finish

L—R: 836 Foal; 1014 Rearing Horse; 815 Foal

1265 Arab Xayal in five different colours

2065	'Arkle' Racehorse on wood base	$11\frac{7}{8}$	139·00	15	1966	C
2084	'Arkle' Racehorse on wood base Pat Taaffe up	$12\frac{5}{8}$	165-185		1966	1980
2137	Tang Horse	8	150-175		1967	1972
2186	Quarter Horse	$8\frac{1}{4}$	55-60		1968	1982
2205	Tang Horse on base	13	250-275		1968	1972
2210	Highwayman on rearing horse (Base set in wood stand)	$13\frac{7}{8}$	300-350		1968	1975
2242	Arab Horse on base	$8\frac{1}{2}$	125-150		1968	1975
2269	Arab Stallion with saddle (on base)	$9\frac{1}{2}$	200-250		1969	1973
2275	Mounted Bedouin Arab (Base set in wood stand)	$11\frac{1}{2}$	300-350		1969	1973
2282	Norwegian Fjord Horse	$6\frac{1}{4}$	125-150		1969	1975
2309	'Burnham Beauty' (Shire Horse also in working harness)	$10\frac{3}{4}$	55-65		1970	1982
2340	'Cardigan Bay' Racehorse on base	$9\frac{1}{4}$	300-350		1970	1976
2345	'Nijinsky' Racehorse on base	$11\frac{1}{8}$	139·00	16	1970	C
2352	'Nijinsky' Racehorse on wood base. Lester Piggott up	$12\frac{5}{8}$	175-195		1971	1982
2421	The Winner Racehorse	$9\frac{3}{4}$	100-120		1972	1982
2422	'Mill Reef' Racehorse on base	9	100-120		1972	1989
2431	Mountie Stallion on base	10	175-200		1972	1975
2459	Mare lying	5	100-125		1973	1976
2460	Foal lying	$3\frac{1}{2}$	50-60		1973	1976
2464	Percheron in show harness	$9\frac{3}{4}$	175-200		1973	1982
2465	Clydesdale in show or working harness	$10\frac{3}{4}$	125-150		1973	1982
†2466	'Black Beauty' Horse	$7\frac{1}{8}$	37·00	65	1973	C
2467	Lippizzaner with Rider on round or oval base	10	200-250		1973	1980
2468	Icelandic Pony	—	100-125		1973	1974
2505	Steeplechaser on base	$8\frac{3}{4}$	200-250		1974	1980
2510	'Red Rum' Racehorse on wood base	12	139·00	18	1974	C
2511	'Red Rum' Racehorse on wood base B. Fletcher Up	$12\frac{1}{4}$	165-185		1974	1983
2535	'Psalm' Racehorse on wood base Anne Moore Up	$12\frac{3}{4}$	145-165		1975	1982
†2536	'Black Beauty' Foal	$5\frac{7}{8}$	15·95	66	1975	C
2540	'Psalm' Racehorse on wood base	$11\frac{1}{2}$	100-120		1975	1982
2541	Welsh Mountain Pony on wood base	9	120-140		1975	1989
2558	'Grundy' Racehorse on wood base	$11\frac{1}{4}$	139·00	20	1976	C
2562	Life-Guard on horseback on wood base	$14\frac{1}{2}$	325·00	22	1976	C

Horses, Foals and Ponies continues after Gallery section

**Higher price for matt finish   †Current models matt only

Gallery

Kangaroo. Models 2312 (small) and 1160 (large)

Racoon Model 2194 and Beaver Model 2195

*Zebra Model **1845** and Zebra (CM Series) Model **1465**.*

*Pig and Pilett Model **2746** and Duck on Skis Model **762***

*Puppit Dog Model **1002***

*L–R **1534** Seal; Polar Bear **1533**; Penguin Family, Two Penguins **1015***

***939** Girl Riding Horse*

Poodle Model **2108**

Bull Terriers Models **970** *(large) and* **1753** *(small)*

*Dachshund and Bulldog (CM Series) Models **1469** and **1463***

*Sealyham Model **971***

*Dubonnet Set: Models **1869–1872**: Bass Ewer Jug Model **2506***

Atlantic Salmon **1233**; *Oceanic Bonito* **1232**

Bunratty Castle Model **2670**

L–R **118** *Mr Pickwick (sugar);* **2099** *Henry VIII;* **2075** *Betsy Trotwood;* **2095** *Falstaff;* **2032** *Mr Bumble;* **372** *Scrooge;* **2031** *Little Nell's Grandmother;* **310** *Mr Micawber*

L–R **1226** *Pheasant;* **1022** *Doves;* **2978** *Pair of Pheasants;* **1219** *Jay;* **2063** *Pair of Grouse;* **1958** *Turkey;* **1218** *Green Woodpecker*

*Kookaburra, Barn Owl and Kingfisher Models **1159, 3273** and **3275***

*Mallard Model **902***   *Jay Model **1219***

"Playtime" Model **1886/3093**

"Sharing" Model **1460/1436**

61

A catalogue page showing character pieces added to the range between 1938 and 1948

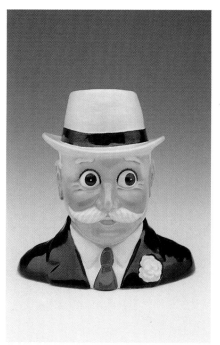

*Beswick Lamp with Model **374** Honey Girl and two Anglund Children Models **2293** and **2272***

Peters Griffin Character Jug

*"A Good Read" Model **2529***

*Dog with Bone Model **1738***

*Whisky Owls Models L–R **2826/1**, **2781**, **2809**, **2825** and **2826/2***

*Figures L–R **1093** Hiker Boy, **437** Girl with Flared Dress and **1122** Butcher Boy*

*Colin Melbourne Model **1411** "Clown on Horse" and **868** "Huntsman on White Horse"*

Catalogue Specials. "Watch It" and "Jennys Baby" with Special Commission "Unicorn"

Model	Description	Size	Price	No.	From	To
†2578	Shire Horse with or without working harness	$8\frac{1}{4}$	55·00	62	1976	C
2582	Blues and Royals on horseback on wood base	$14\frac{1}{2}$	325·00	25	1987	C
2605	Morgan Horse on wood base	$11\frac{1}{2}$	119·00	28	1977	C
2608	'The Minstrel' Racehorse on wood base	$13\frac{1}{4}$	139·00	31	1978	C
2671	'Moonlight' White Racehorse on base	$11\frac{1}{4}$	95·00	35	1980	C
2671	'Sunburst' Palomino	$11\frac{1}{4}$	95·00	36	1986	C
2671	'Nightshade' Black horse	$11\frac{1}{4}$	65-75		1986	1989
2674	'Troy' Racehorse on base	$11\frac{3}{4}$	139·00	37	1980	C
**2688	'Spirit of the Wind' with or without wood base	8	29·95	57	1980	C
**2689	'Spirit of Freedom' with or without wood base	7	29·95	58	1980	C
†2689 &2536	'Spirit of Affection' Black Beauty Foal & Spirit of Freedom together on wood base	7	65·00	64	1980	C
2699	'Troy' head only on wood plaque	6	20-25		1980	1989
2700	'Arkle' head only on wood plaque	6	20-25		1980	1989
2701	'The Minstrel' head only on wood plaque	6	20-25		1981	1989
2702	'Red Rum' head only on wood plaque	6	20-25		1981	1989
**2703	'Spirit of Youth' with or without wood base (same model as 2466)	7	29·95	59	1981	C
**2829	'Spirit of Fire' with or without wood base	8	29·95	60	1983	C
†2837	'Springtime' (foal) on wood base	$4\frac{1}{2}$	18-20	69	1983	C
†2839	'Young Spirit' (foal) on wood base	$4\frac{1}{2}$	18-20	70	1983	C
†2875	'Sunlight' (foal) on wood base	$4\frac{1}{2}$	18-20	71	1985	C
†2876	'Adventure' (foal) on wood base	$4\frac{1}{2}$	18-20	72	1985	C
**2914	'Spirit of Earth' with or without wood base	$7\frac{3}{4}$	40-50	61	1985	C
†2916	'Spirit of Peace' lying with or without wood base	5	40-50	63	1985	C
†2935	'Spirit of Nature' with or without wood base	$5\frac{1}{2}$	49·95	73	1985	C
3021	Cream Unicorn on china base (very limited issue. Special Commission)	$9\frac{1}{4}$	200-250		1987 only	

**Higher price for matt finish   †Current models matt only

Wild Animals
(All current Wild Animals carry a Beswick backstamp)

A trip to the zoo is an exciting day out for all the family and it would appear that the Beswick modellers have also been frequent visitors. The Lion and the Cheetah in the Connoisseur series were both modelled from animals at Dudley Zoo and the Panda (2613) was based on Chi-Chi at London Zoo.

There are over one hundred and thirty different models of which the largest and most spectacular must surely be the Indian Elephant with a tiger clawing its back and the smallest, the Mouse (1678). In between these there is a veritable Noah's Ark of very good quality, finely detailed animals. British wildlife and exotic species have co-existed in the collection over the years, giving animal lovers opportunities to specialise in either field. The Beswick modellers' interpretations have ranged from whimsical, as in the cuddly Panda (1815) to realistic, as in the superbly detailed Connoisseur collection. Various different finishes have been offered in the Wild Animal collection, matt or glossy or, as in some of the earliest models, an all over blue glaze. Although these may lack the naturalism of later wild animals, they are still very appealing to collectors.

Model No	Name of Model	Height inches	Value £	Design Date	Withdrawn By
315	Squirrel on base	8¾	75-100	1935	1954
316	Rabbit on base	6¾	75-100	1935	1954
360	Seal ash bowl	5¾	75-100	1936	1954
368	Frog on base	6	75-100	1936	1954
383	Seal on base	10	75-100	1936	1954
397	Monkey on base	7	75-100	1936	1954
417	Polar Bear on base	6¼	75-100	1936	1954
455	Rabbit bookend	5½	35-40	1936	1954
568	Elephant	9	75-100	1938	1954
569	Elephant	4¾	50-75	1938	1954
692	Elephant	4¼	50-75	1939	1954
696	Fawn standing on base Also in Flambé	7½	75-100	1939	1954
709	Beaver	—	75-100	1939	1954
711	Panda	4½	45-50	1939	1940
720	Panda Baby	3¾	35-40	1939	1954
721	Fawn lying on base	4½	75-100	1939	1954
738	Panda Mother	4½	45-50	1939	1954
823	Rabbit	3	10-15	1940	1971
824	Rabbit	2¼	10-15	1940	1971
825	Rabbit	1⅜	5-10	1940	1971
826	Rabbit	2	5-10	1940	1971
828/1	Elephant	3	40-45	1940	1960
828/2	Elephant	4½	45-50	1940	1960
828/3	Elephant	6	50-60	1940	1960
830	Lizard	7	50-60	1940	1954
841	Leopard sitting	6½	75-100	1940	1954
845	Zebra	7¼	75-100	1940	1969
853	Giraffe	7¼	75-100	1940	1975
954	Stag lying	5½	45-50	1941	1975

974	Elephant	$4\frac{3}{4}$	19·95	1942	C
981	Stag	8	19·95	1942	C
998	Elephant	$10\frac{1}{4}$	150-175	1943	1975
999	Doe	6	19·95	1943	C
1000	Fawn (re-modelled 1955)	$3\frac{1}{2}$	9·95	1943	C
1007	Squirrel standing	$2\frac{1}{4}$	40-45	1944	1967
1008	Squirrel lying	$1\frac{3}{4}$	20-25	1944	1967
1009	Squirrel cracking nut	$4\frac{1}{2}$	20-25	1944	1967
1016	Fox standing	$5\frac{1}{2}$	19·95	1945	C
1017	Fox lying	$1\frac{3}{4}$	9·95	1945	C
1019	Bison	$5\frac{3}{4}$	75-85	1945	1973
1021	Stoat in winter or summer coat	$5\frac{1}{2}$	100-150	1945	1973
1024	Hare running on base	$5\frac{1}{4}$	100-150	1945	1973
1025	Hare sitting	7	100-150	1945	1973
1038	Koala Bear	$3\frac{1}{2}$	20-25	1945	1971
1039	Koala Bear	$2\frac{1}{4}$	15-20	1945	1972
1040	Koala Bear	$2\frac{1}{4}$	15-20	1945	1972
1043	Camel Foal	5	50-60	1946	1971
1044	Camel	7	75-100	1946	1972
1048	Springbok	$7\frac{1}{4}$	150-200	1946	1967
1082	Leopard	$4\frac{3}{4}$	50-60	1946	1975
1089	Koala Bear	$3\frac{1}{2}$	20-25	1947	1971
1160	Kangaroo	$5\frac{3}{4}$	75-100	1949	1967
1308	Skunk	$2\frac{3}{4}$	50-60	1953	1967
1309	Skunk	$1\frac{1}{2}$	30-35	1953	1967
1310	Skunk	2	30-35	1953	1967
1313	Bear (on all fours)	$2\frac{1}{2}$	40-45	1953	1973
1314	Bear standing	$4\frac{1}{2}$	40-45	1953	1973
1315	Baby Bear sitting	$2\frac{1}{4}$	30-35	1953	1973
1409	Bison (CM series)	$7\frac{1}{2}$	75-85	1956	1970
1414	Bison small (CM series)	$5\frac{5}{8}$	60-70	1956	1970
1418	Fox (CM series)	$2\frac{1}{8}$	40-45	1956	1970
1419	Lion (CM series)	$5\frac{1}{4}$	75-85	1956	1970
1440	Fox (small)	$2\frac{1}{2}$	8·95	1956	C
1465	Zebra (CM series)	6	65-75	1956	1970
1468	Bison (CM series)	—	65-75	1956	1970
1475	Fox (CM series)	10 long	65-75	1957	1970
1481	Reindeer (CM series)	$5\frac{1}{2}$	75-85	1957	1970
1486	Tigress	$4\frac{1}{4}$	50-60	1957	1975
1506	Lion (face to front)	$5\frac{1}{4}$	45-50	1957	1965
1507	Lioness	$4\frac{3}{4}$	45-50	1957	1965
1508	Lion Cub	$3\frac{3}{4}$	30-35	1957	1965
1532	Hippopotamus	$3\frac{1}{2}$	75-85	1958	1965
1533	Polar Bear	$4\frac{3}{4}$	75-85	1958	1967
1534	Seal	3	65-75	1958	1967
1551	Chamois	4	20-25	1958	1971
1597	Baby Giraffe	$4\frac{1}{4}$	25-30	1959	1971
1631	Giraffe (large)	12	125-150	1959	1975
1678	Mouse (see 1677 Cats)	$2\frac{1}{2}$	4·95	1960	C
1688	Reindeer	$3\frac{3}{4}$	20-25	1960	1971
1702	Puma, tawny, on rock	$8\frac{1}{2}$	90-100	1960	1989
	Also in Black		100-125	1960	1975
1720	Indian Elephant & Tiger	12	300-350	1960	1975
1748	Fox sitting	3	8·95	1961	C
1770	Indian Elephant as model 1720)	12	150-175	1961	1982

1720 *Indian Elephant and Tiger*

2613 *and* **1815** *Pandas*

1815	Panda	$2\frac{1}{4}$	6·95	1962	C
1823	Puma , tawny, on rock (small)	6	80-90	1962	1975
1943	Beaver	$2\frac{1}{2}$	75-100	1964	1965
2089	Lion (face to side)	$5\frac{1}{2}$	40-45	1967	1983
2090	Moose	$6\frac{1}{4}$	150-200	1966	1973
2093	Old Staffordshire Lion	$5\frac{3}{4}$	100-150	1967	1969
2094	Old Staffordshire Unicorn	6	100-150	1967	1969
2096	Tiger	$7\frac{1}{2}$	40-45	1967	1989
2097	Lioness	$5\frac{3}{4}$	40-45	1967	1983
2098	Lion Cub	4	20-25	1967	1982
2182	Heraldic Unicorn on base	$8\frac{1}{2}$	100-150	1968	1969
2194	Racoon	$4\frac{1}{4}$	125-150	1968	1973
2195	Beaver	$4\frac{3}{8}$	125-150	1968	1973
2222	Lion with crown	$5\frac{1}{4}$	100-150	1968	1969
2223	Unicorn	$5\frac{1}{4}$	100-150	1968	1969
2253	Hedgehog	$3\frac{1}{2}$	35-40	1969	1971
2302	Mouse (see 2301 Cats)	$1\frac{3}{4}$	25-30	1969	1971
2312	Kangaroo (small)	$4\frac{7}{8}$	100-125	1970	1971
2348	Fox	$12\frac{1}{4}$	125-150	1970	1983
2554	Lion	$6\frac{1}{2}$	49·95	1983	C
*2613	Panda 'Chi-Chi' with bamboo shoot	$3\frac{3}{4}$	50-55	1978	1980
2629	Stag	$13\frac{1}{2}$	149·00	1978	C
2725	Cheetah on Rock	$6\frac{1}{2}$	149·00	1981	C
2933	Lion Head	6	20-25	1985	1989
2934	Tiger Head	6	20-25	1985	1989
2936	Stag Head	6	20-25	1985	1989
**2944	Panda sitting	$3\frac{3}{4}$	20-25	1986	1987
3009	Cheetah	5	39·95	1986	C

*for London Zoo   ** for W.W.F

*845 Zebra; **1160** Kangaroo; 853 Giraffe*

Factory Processes

Still Going Strong in 1992 (Courtesy of Royal Doulton)

Fettling

Ready for Decoration

Where is the next spot going?

Part Two: Character Wares

Character and Toby Jugs, Teapots and Derivatives

(All these models carry a Beswick backstamp)

The idea of modelling a jug in the form of a human head is a very ancient one and it occurs with regularity throughout the history of ceramics. In the early 1930s there was a revival of interest in the face jug pioneered by the Royal Doulton potteries and the Beswick modellers were quick to respond to this new collecting interest. Their first character jug, **Tony Weller**, was introduced in 1935 and other Dickens personalities soon followed. During the war some patriotic character jugs were produced, promoting the endeavours of the army, navy and airforce but the Dickens theme was resumed after hostilities had ended. In 1967 two Shakespearean characters joined the throng but production was short lived.

The Beswick character jugs had all been withdrawn by 1973 but the skills of the craftsmen involved have not gone to waste. Today the Beswick studio, as part of the Royal Doulton group, is responsible for the production of all the Character and Toby Jugs with a Royal Doulton backstamp.

Toby Jugs

The Toby differs from the character jug in that the whole figure is modelled into jug form not just the head and shoulders. The Toby has become a popular ornament in the drinking houses of Britain and is highly valued by many collectors. Of the six very attractive models which Beswick have produced, three are traditional types in which Toby Phillpot, a character in a popular eighteenth century drinking song, sits with a jug of ale in one hand and a tankard in the other.

The topers were soon joined by other congenial characters. **The Midshipman** playing the violin was a popular subject in the 1770s and Beswick produced a faithful version of him in 1948. The **Martha Gunn** Toby was also inspired by an eighteenth century original by Ralph Wood. She was the bathing attendant at Brighton beach who supposedly taught King George IV to swim.

Famous characters of the twentieth century have also been portrayed in Toby form and **Winston Churchill** has probably been most 'honoured' in this way. During the war Beswick introduced a very fine image of him which was only available until 1954.

All of these jugs can be classed as rare and are very hard to find today.

Derivatives

The popular Dickens personalities were not confined to character jugs. It was possible to deck out the tea table with useful Dickens wares — a **Dolly Varden** teapot with perhaps a **Pecksniff** cream jug and a **Pickwick** sugar bowl. Jam could be discreetly contained in a **Tony Weller** preserve pot and for extra spice the **Sairey Gamp** pepper pot and **Mr Micawber** salt pot could be on hand. These were all the specialities of Mr Gredington who offered alternative favourite characters.

It is doubtful whether any of these entertaining characters serve their original purpose today as they are now much sought after by collectors.

Model No	Name of Model		Height inches	Value £	Design Date	Withdrawn By
281	Tony Weller (1st version)	CJ	$6\frac{3}{4}$	50-60	1935	1973
281	Tony Weller (2nd version)	CJ	7	65-70	1969	1973
310	Micawber (1st version)	CJ	$8\frac{1}{4}$	50-60	1935	1973
310	Micawber (2nd version)	CJ	$8\frac{1}{2}$	65-70	1969	1973
371	Sairey Gamp	CJ	$6\frac{1}{2}$	50-60	1936	1973
372	Scrooge	CJ	7	50-60	1936	1973
575	Laurel & Hardy cruet & base		$4\frac{1}{2}$	35-40	1938	1969
673	Tony Weller sugar		$2\frac{3}{4}$	20-25	1939	1973
674	Mr Micawber cream		$3\frac{1}{4}$	15-20	1939	1973

1203 Dolly Varden and *1369* Sam Weller teapots

689	Sairey Gamp pepper		2½	15-20	1939	1973
690	Mr Micawber salt		3½	15-20	1939	1973
691	Sairey Gamp teapot		5¾	60-65	1939	1973
735	Old Bill	CJ	5	140-160	1939	1954
736	Navy	CJ	5	140-160	1939	1954
737	Air Force	CJ	5	140-160	1939	1954
742	Panda teapot		6	90-100	1939	1954
931	Winston Churchill	TJ	7	200-250	1941	1954
1110	Toby Phillpot	TJ	8	75-85	1948	1973
1111	Toby Phillpot	TJ	6½	65-75	1948	1973
1112	Midshipman Toby	TJ	5¼	125-150	1948	1973
1113	Martha Gunn holding jug	TJ	3½	100-125	1948	1966
1114	Toby Sitting on Barrel holding jug	TJ	3½	100-125	1948	1966
1116	Peggoty teapot		6	70-75	1948	1973
1117	Pecksniff cream		3½	15-20	1948	1973
1118	Pickwick sugar		3	15-20	1948	1973
1119	Pickwick cream		3¼	15-20	1948	1973
1120	Captain Cuttle	CJ	4½	40-45	1948	1973
1121	Barnaby Rudge	CJ	4½	40-45	1948	1969
1129	Pecksniff sugar		3½	15-20	1948	1973
1203	Dolly Varden teapot		6¼	90-100	1950	1973
1204	Mr Varden cream		3½	15-20	1950	1973
1205	Mrs Varden sugar		3	20-25	1950	1973
1206	Sairey Gamp preserve & lid		3	25-30	1950	1973
1207	Tony Weller preserve & lid		3	25-30	1950	1973
1369	Sam Weller teapot		6¼	100-120	1955	1973
2030	Martin Chuzzlewit	CJ	4¾	50-60	1965	1973
2031	Little Nell's Grandfather	CJ	5⅜	50-60	1965	1973
2032	Mr Bumble	CJ	4⅞	50-60	1965	1973
2075	Betsy Trotwood	CJ	5	50-60	1966	1973
2095	Falstaff	CJ	6¾	65-75	1965	1973
2099	Henry VIII	CJ	7	65-75	1967	1973
3105	Panda teapot		6	25-30	1989	1990
3138	Cat teapot		6	25-30	1989	1990
3139	Mouse teapot		7	25-30	1989	1990
3142	Squirrel teapot		7	25-30	1989	1990

CJ Character Jug   TJ Toby Jug

L—R: **737** Air Force; **735** Old Bill; **736** Navy. (Courtesy of the Toby Jug China Shop, Blackheath)

1301 Nana

Walt Disney Group

1104 Little Pig Robinson variations

1365 Pigling Bland variations

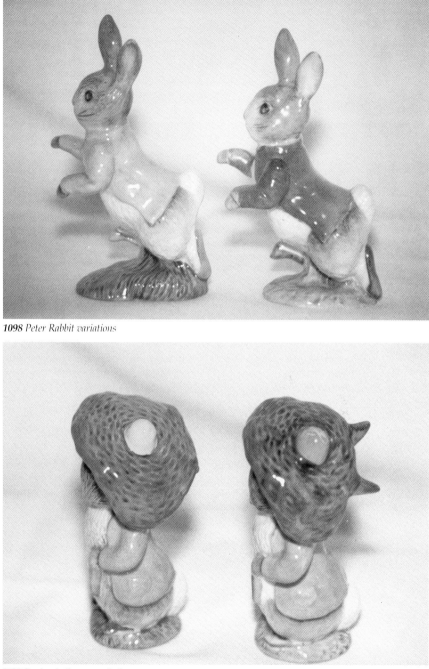

1098 Peter Rabbit variations

1105 Benjamin Bunny variations

Characters from Film and Literature

(All models produced up to August 1989 carry a Beswick stamp. All current models produced since August 1989 carry a Royal Albert stamp)

Over the years, the Beswick modellers have turned the pages of many children's classics and brought a new dimension to the memorable illustrations, so that as well as enjoying the books, young readers could surround themselves with little models of their favourite characters. The timeless quality of many Victorian and Edwardian children's books makes them a fertile source of inspiration and Beswick modellers have had particular success with their interpretations of Alice in Wonderland and the tales of Beatrix Potter.

The first Beatrix Potter figure was suggested by Mrs Lucy Beswick, wife of Ewart, when she mentioned to Jim Hayward in 1947 that Jemima Puddleduck might be a good subject for a figure. When Jim Hayward took up her suggestion, copies of the Beatrix Potter tales belonging to her daughter Judith soon disappeared into the design studio. The result was so successful that a whole range of character studies from the tales of Beatrix Potter followed.

This extract from **The Publishers' Circular and Booksellers' Record** of July 1950 gives an indication of the popularity of the Beatrix Potter figures: "These little figures are creating a buying craze which is sweeping through the United States of America and Canada. This well known pottery firm first issued twelve of these charming china figures, each being about three and three quarter inches high, beautifully fashioned and coloured after the famous illustrations from Beatrix Potter's works. The colourings are full, the figures most natural and the whole present beautiful objects d'art."

Today a new figure may be suggested from the illustrations in the books — perhaps a popular character such as Peter Rabbit or Benjamin Bunny in a change of clothes or a different pose. Alternatively, the name of a character not previously illustrated such as Cottontail might suggest a study for designers in the studio. Any new ideas are discussed by the design manager and the modeller and several drawings and trial models follow. The figure must agree with the original book illustrations in every detail and so meticulous is the process that it can take six months or even longer for a model to be completed.

Following the success of the Beatrix Potter figures, Beswick started to introduce other characters from literature and film. In 1949 they introduced Zimmy the Lion, the star of **The Lion** cartoon released by the Rank Film Organisation in 1948. This character was the creation of David Hand, an ex-director at Walt Disney and such was Zimmy's success with his audience that sequel cartoons soon appeared introducing his friends Ginger Nutt, Hazel Nutt, Dinkum Platypus, Loopy Hare, Oscar Ostrich and Dusty Mole. Arthur Gredington added all these cartoon characters to the Beswick collection.

In 1952, the most famous cartoon character of all, Walt Disney's Mickey Mouse, was portrayed by Miss Granoska. Such was the popularity of Mickey and his friends that these Beswick figures are now very hard to find indeed in spite of being in production for twelve years. Also elusive are Snow White and the Seven Dwarfs which were introduced in 1954.

It was fourteen years before Beswick returned to the world of children for inspiration. Prompted by the success of Walt Disney's film version of A. A. Milne's **Winnie the Pooh**, Albert Hallam modelled a series of characters in 1968. Pooh Bear himself and Piglet must be the best known of this group along with Christopher Robin, a central character in all the books. All of these figures are now out of production and their appealing modelling makes them well worth collecting.

Another famous bear portrayed by Beswick was originally created by Mary Tourtel in 1920 but it was Alfred Bestall who popularised him in the first **Rupert Annual** published by the **Daily Express** newspaper in 1936. All of the stories and drawings in this annual were the work of Alfred Bestall who continued to write illustrated stories every year until 1973. Rupert Bear and his friends Algy Pug and Bill Badger were introduced in 1980 and have now been withdrawn.

One of the best known children's classics which has inspired the Beswick artists is **Alice's Adventures in Wonderland** by Lewis Carroll. It would seem that they referred to the original drawings by John Tenniel in the 1865 edition of this book when creating their set of eleven colourful characters. The Mad Hatter and Alice herself are particularly attractive and difficult to find.

Unlike the characters from Alice in Wonderland, Beatrix Potter and Rupert Bear, Beswick's Thelwell collection is not based on illustrations from children's stories but on a series of cartoons for **Punch** magazine. The girl and pony theme of Norman Thelwell's drawings was inspired by an incident he observed from his window. Two small podgy girls, hard hats rammed down over their ears, approached a shaggy pony well known for his uncertain temper. They calmly marched towards him, pulled his tail, cracked his nose with a crop and so made the pony their obedient servant before his astonishment had time to turn to fury. The Beswick models, first introduced in 1982 and modelled by David Lyttleton, capture the humour portrayed in Thelwell's pony cartoons.

The Beswick artists have had a long standing ability to portray character and humour and this is very much in evidence, not only in the Thelwell collection but in all their portrayals of characters from children's stories and cartoons.

Another children's classic has been interpreted by the Beswick modellers, but for various reasons the series was only available for between two and three years.

The four main characters in Kenneth Graham's story The Wind in the Willows, were Toad, Badger, Mole and Ratty and models of each were introduced in 1987, to be followed by Portly (Otter) and Weasel Gamekeeper in 1988. They were all withdrawn at the end of 1989.

The Royal Albert backstamp was used and each figure was allocated a model number in the Beswick pattern book. Details are given in the listings, together with the Royal Albert number.

This set came out at the same time as the decision was made, by Royal Doulton, to change the backstamp of Beatrix Potter figures from Beswick to Royal Albert.

It is probable that this Brand name was thought to have more appeal, particularly to overseas markets.

The actual changeover date was set at 1st August, 1989, but it was obviously going to take some time for existing Beswick-marked models to clear the factory warehouse and be replaced by Royal Albert marked models.

It is believed that the highest number B.P. model to carry the Beswick mark is 3103, Tom Kitten character jug and the highest number figure to be 3094, Johnny Townmouse and Bag.

Model number 3157, Peter in the Gooseberry Net, is therefore the first B.P. model never to have carried the Beswick stamp.

In the listings, all B.P. models, from 3157 onwards, carry the Royal Albert mark and the number quoted is the Beswick pattern book model number. This number is also used in the currently published price list.

There are, however three exceptions. Due to delayed production, B.P. models 2965/66/71 were not introduced until after the backstamp changes had been made and they have therefore only carried the Royal Albert mark.

The popular Beswick gold backstamp was in use until 1970, when the brown printed transfer was substituted. It is believed that 2334 Pickles is the highest numbered model to carry a gold backstamp. These older, but still current models command a higher price.

In 1987 the three new BP character jugs models 2959/2960/3006 had a new style of backstamp where the printed word "BESWICK" was replaced by the written words John Beswick.

In 1988 the three new BP character jugs 3088/3102/3103 and three new BP figures 3090/3091/3094 all had a different style of backstamp, where the written words John Beswick were followed by the printed words "STUDIO OF ROYAL DOULTON, ENGLAND".

The other three new BP figures introduced in 1988 — 2989/2996/3030 — all carried the standard printed "BESWICK" mark. All now carry the Royal Albert stamp.

Model No	Name of Model		Height inches	Value £	Design Date	Withdrawn By
857	Alice & White Rabbit on base	AIW	—	75-90	1940	1950
858	Dormouse &Alice plaque	AIW	—	75-90	1940	1950
859	King& Alice plaque	AIW	—	75-90	1940	1950
860	Alice playing croquet on base	AIW	—	75-90	1940	1950

*Duchess Models **1355** and **2601***

Beatrix Potter character group

861	Cinderella feeding birds plaque	—		75-90	1940	1950
863	Cinderella dressing the ugly sisters plaque	—		75-90	1940	1950
865	Cinderella running from the ball plaque	—		75-90	1940	1950
866	Cinderella & slipper plaque	—		75-90	1940	1950
867	The Prince finds Cinderella plaque	—		75-90	1940	1950
1092/1	Jemima Puddleduck (2in short base)	BP	$4\frac{1}{4}$	20-25	1947	1989
1092/2	Jemima Puddleduck (2$\frac{1}{4}$in long base)	BP	$4\frac{1}{4}$	12·95	1989	C
1098/1	Peter Rabbit (2in short base)	BP	$4\frac{1}{2}$	20-25	1947	1989
1098/2	Peter Rabbit (2$\frac{3}{8}$in long base)	BP	$4\frac{1}{2}$	12·95	1989	C
1100	Tom Kitten	BP	$3\frac{1}{2}$	12·95	1947	C
1101	Timmy Tiptoes	BP	$3\frac{3}{4}$	12·95	1947	C
1102	Squirrel Nutkin	BP	$3\frac{3}{4}$	12·95	1947	C
1103	Mrs Tittlemouse	BP	$3\frac{3}{4}$	12·95	1947	C
1104/1	Little Pig Robinson (Blue striped smock)	BP	4	40-50	1947	1983
1104/2	Little Pig Robinson (Blue checked smock)	BP	4	12·95	1983	C
1105/1	Benjamin Bunny (left arm & slipper held away & ears protrude beyond hat)	BP	4	100-125	1947	1979
1105/2	Benjamin Bunny (left arm & slipper flush to body & ears protrude beyond hat)	BP	4	100-125	1979	1983
1105/3	Benjamin Bunny (left arm & slipper flush to body & ears do not protrude)	BP	4	12·95	1983	C
1106	Samuel Whiskers	BP	$3\frac{1}{2}$	12·95	1947	C
1107/1	Mrs Tiggy Winkle (angled stripes to blouse)	BP	$3\frac{1}{4}$	40-50	1947	1975
1107/2	Mrs Tiggy Winkle (vertical stripes to blouse)	BP	$3\frac{1}{4}$	12·95	1975	C
1108	Tailor of Gloucester	BP	$3\frac{3}{4}$	12·95	1948	C
1109	Timmy Willie	BP	3	12·95	1948	C
1148	Dinkum Platypus	DHA	$4\frac{1}{4}$	75-100	1949	1955
1150	Zimmy Lion	DHA	$3\frac{3}{4}$	100-125	1949	1955
1151	Felia Cat	DHA	4	100-125	1949	1955
1152	Ginger Nutt	DHA	4	100-125	1949	1955
1153	Hazel Nutt	DHA	$3\frac{3}{4}$	100-125	1949	1955
1154	Oscar Ostrich	DHA	$3\frac{3}{4}$	100-125	1949	1955
1155	Dusty Mole	DHA	$3\frac{1}{2}$	100-125	1949	1955
1156	Loopy Hare	DHA	$4\frac{1}{4}$	100-125	1949	1955
1157/1	Jeremy Fisher (spotted body)	BP	3	40-50	1949	1979
1157/2	Jeremy Fisher (striped body)	BP	3	12·95	1979	C

1183	Lady Mouse	BP	4	12·95	1950	C
1198	Hunca Munca	BP	$2\frac{3}{4}$	12·95	1950	C
1199	Mrs Ribby	BP	$3\frac{1}{2}$	12·95	1950	C
1200/1	Mrs Rabbit (brolly sticks out)	BP	$4\frac{1}{4}$	100-125	1950	1983
1200/2	Mrs Rabbit (brolly flush to body)	BP	$4\frac{1}{4}$	12·95	1983	C
1274	Flopsy, Mopsy & Cottontail	BP	$2\frac{3}{4}$	12·95	1952	C
1275	Miss Moppet	BP	3	12·95	1952	C
1276	Johnny Townmouse	BP	$3\frac{1}{2}$	12·95	1952	C
1277	Foxy Whiskered Gentleman	BP	5	12·95	1952	C
1278	Mickey Mouse	WD	$3\frac{7}{8}$	125-150	1952	1965
1279	Jiminy Cricket	WD	4	125-150	1952	1965
1280	Pluto	WD	$3\frac{1}{2}$	125-150	1953	1965
1281	Goofy	WD	$4\frac{1}{4}$	125-150	1953	1965
1282	Pinocchio	WD	4	125-150	1953	1965
1283	Donald Duck	WD	4	125-150	1953	1965
1289	Minnie Mouse	WD	4	125-150	1953	1965
1291	Thumper	WD	$3\frac{3}{4}$	125-150	1953	1965
1301	Nana	WD	$3\frac{1}{4}$	125-150	1953	1965
1302	Smee	WD	$4\frac{1}{8}$	125-150	1953	1965
1307	Peter Pan	WD	5	125-150	1953	1965
1312	Tinkerbell	WD	5	125-150	1953	1965
1325	Dopey	WD	$3\frac{1}{2}$	100-125	1954	1967
1326	Happy	WD	$3\frac{1}{2}$	100-125	1954	1967
1327	Bashful	WD	$3\frac{1}{2}$	100-125	1954	1967
1328	Sneezy	WD	$3\frac{1}{2}$	100-125	1954	1967
1329	Doc	WD	$3\frac{1}{2}$	100-125	1954	1967
1330	Grumpy	WD	$3\frac{1}{2}$	100-125	1954	1967
1331	Sleepy	WD	$3\frac{1}{2}$	100-125	1954	1967
1332	Snow White	WD	5	300-350	1954	1967
1348/1	Tommy Brock (spade handle above hand)	BP	$3\frac{1}{2}$	50-60	1954	1979
1348/2	Tommy Brock (spade handle flush with hand)	BP	$3\frac{1}{2}$	12·95	1979	C
1355	Duchess (see also 2601)	BP	$3\frac{3}{4}$	250-300	1954	1967
1365/1	Pigling Bland (dark mauve jacket and $1\frac{5}{8}$in dia base)	BP	$4\frac{1}{4}$	40-50	1955	1980
1365/2	Pigling Bland (pale violet jacket and $1\frac{7}{8}$in dia base)	BP	$4\frac{1}{4}$	12·95	1980	C
1531	Tree lamp base	BP	7	40-50	1958	1982
1545	Old Woman Who Lived in a Shoe	BP	$2\frac{1}{2}$	12·95	1958	C
1675	Goody Tiptoes	BP	$3\frac{1}{2}$	12·95	1960	C
1676/1	Tabitha Twitchett (blue striped "V" neck)	BP	$3\frac{1}{2}$	40-50	1960	1983
1676/2	Tabitha Twitchett (white "V" neck)	BP	$3\frac{1}{2}$	12·95	1983	C
1796	Old Mr Brown	BP	$3\frac{1}{4}$	12·95	1962	C
1851	Anna Maria	BP	3	60-80	1962	1982
1940/1	Mr Benjamin Bunny (left arm & pipe away from body)	BP	$4\frac{1}{4}$	100-125	1964	1975

1940/2	Mr Benjamin Bunny (left arm & pipe moulded into body)	BP	4¼	12·95	1975	C
1941/1	Cecily Parsley (ears up and head down)	BP	4	40-50	1964	1986
1941/2	Cecily Parsley (ears back and head up)	BP	4	12·95	1986	C
1942	Mrs Flopsy Bunny	BP	4	12·95	1964	C
2061	Amiable Guinea Pig	BP	3½	80-100	1966	1982
2082	Jemima Puddleduck Plaque	BP	6	75-100	1966	1969
2083	Peter Rabbit Plaque	BP	6	75-100	1966	1969
2085	Tom Kitten Plaque	BP	6	75-100	1966	1969
2193	Winnie the Pooh	WD	2½	25-30	1968	1990
2196	Eeyore	WD	2	25-30	1968	1990
2214	Piglet	WD	2¾	30-35	1968	1990
2215	Rabbit	WD	3⅛	25-30	1968	1990
2216	Owl	WD	3	25-30	1968	1990
2217	Kanga	WD	3⅛	25-30	1968	1990
2276	Aunt Pettitoes	BP	3¾	12·95	1969	C
2284	Cousin Ribby	BP	3¼	12·95	1969	C
2295	Display Stand	BP	12½ x 2½	13·95	1969	C
2333	Appley Dapply	BP	3¼	12·95	1970	C
2334	Pickles	BP	4½	75-100	1970	1982
2381	Pig-Wig	BP	4	75-100	1971	1982
2394	Tigger	WD	3	30-35	1971	1990
2395	Christopher Robin	WD	4¾	45-50	1971	1990
2424	Mr Alderman Ptolemy	BP	3¾	12·95	1972	C
2425	Sir Isaac Newton	BP	3⅞	100-125	1972	1984
2452	Sally Hennypenny	BP	4	12·95	1973	C
2453/1	Mr Jackson (green)	BP	2¾	60-80	1973	1982
2453/2	Mr Jackson (fawn)	BP	2¾	12·95	1982	C
2476	Alice	AIW	4¾	175-225	1973	1983
2477	White Rabbit	AIW	4¾	175-225	1973	1983
2478	Mock Turtle	AIW	4¼	50-75	1973	1983
2479	Mad Hatter	AIW	4¼	175-225	1973	1983
2480	Cheshire Cat	AIW	1½	200-250	1973	1983
2485	Gryphon	AIW	3¼	50-75	1973	1983
2489	King of Hearts	AIW	3¾	40-50	1973	1983
2490	Queen of Hearts	AIW	4	40-50	1973	1983
2508	Simpkin	BP	4	150-200	1974	1982
2509	Mr Benjamin Bunny & Peter Rabbit	BP	4	19·95	1974	C
2526	A Family Mouse	KM	3⅜	30-40	1975	1983
2527	A Double Act	KM	3⅜	30-40	1975	1983
2528	The Racegoer	KM	3⅜	30-40	1975	1983
2529	A Good Read	KM	2⅝	150-200	1975	1983
2530	Lazy Bones	KM	1⅝	30-40	1975	1983
2531	A Snack	KM	3¼	30-40	1975	1983
2532	Strained Relations	KM	3⅛	30-40	1975	1983
2533	Just Good Friends	KM	3⅛	30-40	1975	1983
2543	Mrs Rabbit & Bunnies	BP	3½	12·95	1975	C
2544	Tabitha Twitchett with Miss Moppett	BP	3½	16·95	1975	C
2545	Dodo	AIW	4	100-125	1975	1983
2546	Fish Footman	AIW	4⅝	100-125	1975	1983
2547	Frog Footman	AIW	4¼	125-150	1975	1983

2559	Ginger	BP	$3\frac{3}{4}$	150-200	1976	1982
2560	Poorly Peter Rabbit	BP	$3\frac{1}{2}$	12·95	1976	C
2565	The Ring	KM	$3\frac{1}{4}$	40-50	1976	1983
2566	Guilty Sweethearts	KM	$2\frac{1}{4}$	50-60	1976	1983
2584	Hunca Munca Sweeping	BP	$3\frac{1}{8}$	12·95	1977	C
2585	Little Black Rabbit	BP	$4\frac{3}{8}$	12·95	1977	C
2586	Fierce Bad Rabbit	BP	$4\frac{3}{4}$	12·95	1977	C
2589	All I Do Is Think of You	KM	$2\frac{3}{8}$	60-80	1977	1983
2594	Jemima Puddleduck & Foxy Whiskered Gentleman Plaque	BP	$7\frac{1}{2} \times 7\frac{1}{2}$	30-40	1977	1982
2601	The Duchess (see also 1355)	BP	4	50-75	1977	1982
2627	Chippy Hackee	BP	$3\frac{3}{4}$	12·95	1978	C
2628	Mr Drake Puddleduck	BP	$4\frac{1}{4}$	12·95	1978	C
2647	Rebeccah Puddleduck	BP	$3\frac{1}{4}$	12·95	1979	C
2650	Peter Rabbit Plaque	BP	$7\frac{1}{2} \times 7\frac{1}{2}$	30-40	1979	1983
2668	Thomasina Tittlemouse	BP	$3\frac{1}{4}$	20-25	1980	1990
2685	Mrs Tittlemouse Plaque	BP	$7\frac{1}{2} \times 7\frac{1}{2}$	35-45	1981	1984
2694	Rupert Bear	R	$4\frac{1}{4}$	140-160	1980	1986
*2704	An Angel on Horseback	T	$4\frac{1}{2}$	45-55	1981	1989
2710	Algy Pug	R	4	50-75	1981	1986
2711	Pong Ping	R	$4\frac{1}{4}$	50-75	1981	1986
2713	Diggory Diggory Delvet	BP	$2\frac{3}{4}$	12·95	1981	C
2716	Susan	BP	$4\frac{1}{2}$	30-35	1981	1990
2720	Bill Badger	R	$2\frac{3}{4}$	50-75	1981	1986
2767	Old Mr Pricklepin	BP	$2\frac{1}{2}$	20-25	1982	1990
*2769	Kick Start	T	$3\frac{1}{2}$	40-55	1982	1989
2779	Rupert Bear snowballing	R	$4\frac{1}{4}$	140-160	1982	1986
*2789	Pony Express	T	$4\frac{1}{2}$	45-55	1982	1989
2803/1	Benjamin Bunny Sat On A Bank (head to side)	BP	$3\frac{3}{4}$	30-40	1982	1987
2803/2	Benjamin Bunny Sat On A Bank (head to front)	BP	$3\frac{3}{4}$	12·95	1987	C
2804	Old Woman Who Lived in a Shoe — knitting	BP	3	12·95	1982	C
2823	Jemima Puddleduck Made A Feather Nest	BP	$2\frac{1}{4}$	12·95	1983	C
2877	Mrs Tiggy Winkle Takes Tea	BP	$3\frac{1}{4}$	12·95	1985	C
2878	Cottontail	BP	$3\frac{1}{2}$	12·95	1985	C
2939	Mole — AW4	WIW	3	20-25	1987	1989
2940	Badger — AW3	WIW	3	20-25	1987	1989
2941	Ratty— AW2	WIW	$3\frac{5}{8}$	20-25	1987	1989
2942	Toad — AW1	WIW	$3\frac{5}{8}$	20-25	1987	1989
2956	Old Mr Bouncer	BP	$2\frac{7}{8}$	12·95	1986	C
2957	Goody and Timmy Tiptoes	BP	4	23·00	1986	C
2959	Old Mr Brown (Character Jug)	BP	$2\frac{1}{2}$	19·95	1987	C
2960	Jeremy Fisher (Character Jug)	BP	$2\frac{3}{4}$	19·95	1987	C

* available in Grey or Bay

2965	John Joiner (Dog)	BP	2½	12·95	1990	C
2966	Mother Ladybird	BP	2½	12·95	1989	C
2971	Babbitty Bumble (Bee)	BP	2¾	12·95	1989	C
2989	Tom Thumb	BP	3	12·95	1988	C
2996	Timmy Willie sleeping	BP	1¾	12·95	1988	C
3006	Peter Rabbit (Character Jug)	BP	2¾	19·95	1988	C
3030	Tom Kitten & Butterfly	BP	3½	14·95	1988	C
3031	Little Pig Robinson spying	BP	3½	15·95	1988	C
3065	Portly (Otter) AW6	WIW	2¾	25-30	1988	1989
3076	Weasel Gamekeeper AW5	WIW	4	25-30	1988	1989
3088	Jemima Puddleduck (Character Jug)	BP	3¼	19·95	1988	
3090	Mr Jeremy Fisher digging	BP	3½	15·95	1988	C
3091	Mr Tod	BP	4¾	15·95	1988	C
3094	Johnny Townmouse with bag	BP	3½	15·95	1988	C
3102	Mrs Tigglewinkle (Character Jug)	BP	3	19·95	1988	C
3103	Tom Kitten (Character Jug)	BP	3	19·95	1988	C
3157	Peter In The Gooseberry Net	BP	2	15·95	1990	C
3193	Jemima Puddleduck with Foxy Whiskered Gentleman	BP	4¾	24·00	1990	C
3197	Mittens & Moppet	BP	3¾	17·95	1990	C
3200	Gentleman Mouse Made A Bow	BP	3	12·95	1990	C
3219	Foxy Reading Country News	BP	4¼	18·50	1990	C
3220	Lady Mouse Made A Curtsy	BP	2¾	12·95	1990	C
3234	Benjamin Wakes Up	BP	2¼	12·95	1991	C
3242	Peter And The Red Pocket Handkerchief	BP	4½	15·95	1991	C
3251	Miss Dormouse	BP	4	19·95	1991	C
3252	Pigling Eats His Porridge	BP	4	15·95	1991	C
3257	Christmas Stocking (Hunca Munca & Wife)	BP	3½	19·95	1991	C
3278	Mrs Rabbit Cooking	BP	4	12·95	1992	C
3280	Ribby & the Patty Pan	BP	3½	12·95	1992	C
3288	Hunca Munca with Beads	BP	3¼	14·95	1992	C
3317	Benjamin Bunny Eats A Lettuce Leaf	BP			1992	C
3319	This Little Pig Had None	BP			1992	C
3325	No More Twist	BP			1992	C

BP Beatrix Potter   WD Walt Disney   DHA David Hand Animaland   T Thelwell
KM Kitty McBride   R Rupert Bear   AIW Alice In Wonderland   C Current
WIW Wind in the Willows (Royal Albert)

Comical Animals and Birds

(All models carry a Beswick backstamp)

Apart from their modelling skills many of the Beswick artists have had another strong asset, a lively sense of humour, and this is reflected in a large number of pieces in the collection. A time-honoured way of raising a smile is to endow an animal with human characteristics, and so it is not surprising to find dogs, cats and monkeys playing musical instruments, a cat hiking, a duck on skis, penguins sporting umbrellas and even a monkey smoking a pipe, one of the most appealing studies in the group. Sometimes facial expressions alone are sufficient to amuse, as with the dog going cross-eyed looking at a ladybird on the end of his nose (804). Occasionally the animals themselves join in the joke — there are laughing pigs, cats and a dog introduced in 1967.

In recent years the Beswick artists have sought comedy in familiar situations such as the cats curled up on chimney pots which form a cruet set in the 'Fun Ceramics' collection or the snoozing pigs in the 'Farmyard Humour' series.

The ability to entertain in this way is an endearing aspect of the Beswick story and hopefully the laughter will continue for many years to come.

Sporting Cats

Model No	Name of Model	Height inches	Value £	Design Date	Withdrawn By
87	Dog Sitting in Armchair book end	7½	35-40	1934	1967
172	Loch Ness Monster	—	25-30	1936	1954
317	Duck on base	8¼	90-100	1936	1955
324	Poodle begging	7	90-100	1936	1954
624	Rabbit with knapsack	4	45-50	1938	1967
663	Elephant with five ton weight	—	45-50	1938	1967
664	Fox with elbow on tree trunk	4½	45-50	1938	1967
665	Rabbit with golf bag	4¾	45-50	1938	1967
688	Teddy bear	—	50-60	1939	1967
697	Hippo Laughing	2¼	45-50	1939	1973
698	Giraffe sizes 1 & 2	—	50-60 each	1939	1970
	size 3	—	40-50	1940	1970
760	Duck with ladybird on nose	3⅞	15-20	1939	1971
761	Dog with bandage	4¼	25-35	1939	1971
762	Duck on skis	3¼	25-35	1939	1969
765	Three Ducks	2¾	20-25	1939	1971
802	Penguin with umbrella up (re-modelled 1956)	4¼	25-30	1940	1972
803	Penguin with walking stick (re-modelled 1956) (Part of set see 800 and 801 in Birds)	3¾	20-25	1940	1972
804	Dog with ladybird on nose	4	15-20	1940	1969
805/1	Dog with ladybird on tail	3¾	15-20	1940	1969
805/2	Dog with ladybird on tail	2½	10-15	1940	1969
811	Dog playing accordian	4	40-45	1940	1970
812	Dog asleep on drum	2⅞	30-35	1940	1970
813	Dog with ladybird on nose	4	15-20	1940	1970
831	Dog with glasses reading book	6¼	50-55	1940	1970
907	Dog with ladybird on tail	3¼	10-15	1941	1971
1001	Cockerel	5¾	75-95	1944	1970
1002	Puppit dog	4¾	40-50	1944	1969
1003	Fawnie	5¼	75-95	1944	1970
1004	Rooster	7	75-95	1944	1973
1005	Kangarinie	5	75-95	1944	1970
1006	Grebie (small duck)	5¼	75-95	1944	1970
1026	Cat orchestra conductor	2	20-25	1945	1972
1027	Cat cellist	2	20-25	1945	1972
1028	Cat violinist	2	20-25	1945	1972
1029	Cat saxophonist	2	20-25	1945	1972
1049	Monkey smoking pipe	4¼	50-60	1946	1969
1054	Dog holding 'My Plate'	4¼	40-50	1947	1967
1058	Dog	4½	40-50	1946	1973
1088	Dog	3½	40-50	1947	1973
1255	Monkey drummer	2⅝	100-125	1952	1973
1256	Monkey tuba player	2⅝	100-125	1952	1973
1257	Monkey fiddler	2⅝	100-125	1952	1973
1258	Monkey saxophonist	2⅝	100-125	1952	1973
1259	Monkey guitarist	2⅝	100-125	1952	1973
1260	Monkey banjo player	2⅝	100-125	1952	1973
1335	Tortoise mother	2¾ long	50-60	1954	1972
1336	Tortoise girl	1¾ long	25-30	1954	1972

*Squirrel Set Models **1007/08/09***

Monkey Band

1337	Tortoise boy	$1\frac{3}{4}$ long	25-30	1954	1972
1379	Bush Baby with mirror	2	40-50	1955	1967
1380	Bush Baby with stud	2	40-50	1955	1967
1381	Bush Baby with candy	$1\frac{1}{2}$	40-50	1955	1967
1733	Fox	$3\frac{1}{4}$	50-60	1961	1966
1738	Pup with bone	$3\frac{3}{4}$	75-100	1961	1967
2100	Cat and mouse laughing	3	60-80	1967	1972
2101	Cat laughing	3	40-60	1967	1972
2102	Dog laughing	$2\frac{7}{8}$	40-60	1967	1972
2103	Two Pigs laughing	$2\frac{3}{4}$	60-80	1967	1972
2130	Dog praying	$2\frac{7}{8}$	40-60	1967	1972
2131	Rabbit yawning	$2\frac{7}{8}$	40-60	1967	1972
2132	Rabbit & baby asleep	$2\frac{7}{8}$	60-80	1967	1971
2200	Chicken running	$1\frac{1}{4}$	25-30	1968	1973
2201	Chicken pecking	1	25-30	1968	1973
2202	Chicken sitting	$1\frac{1}{2}$	25-30	1968	1973
2746	Pig & piglet riding piggy back	$2\frac{3}{4}$	14·95	1981	C
2761	Cat asleep on chimney. Salt, pepper and stand	4	40-60	1982	1986
2792	Daisy the Cow creamer	$5\frac{3}{4}$	25-30	1983	1989
2802	Umbrella money box "Saving for a Rainy Day"	$5\frac{1}{4}$	35-40	1983	1986
2805	Pillar Box money box with cat on top	$6\frac{1}{4}$	35-40	1983	1986
2810	Egg cup with cat	$2\frac{3}{8}$	20-25	1983	1986
*3012	Sporting Cat Footballer in striped colours	$4\frac{1}{8}$	25-35	1987 only	
A	Orange and White				
B	Maroon and White				
C	Black and White				
D	Light Blue and White				
E	Yellow & White				
*3016	Sporting Cat Footballer in plain colours	$4\frac{1}{8}$	25-35	1987 only	
A	Orange and White				
B	Maroon and White				
C	Black and White				
D	Light Blue and White				
E	Yellow & White				
*3023	Sporting Cat Cricketer	$4\frac{1}{8}$			
*3027	Sporting Cat Bowls	$4\frac{1}{8}$			
*3039	Sporting Cat Tennis	$4\frac{1}{8}$			

*In this projected series, only the Footballer Cats were put into limited production.

Figures (All models carry a Beswick backstamp)

Beswick have produced a wide variety of figures. From 1894 they made the traditional Staffordshire types and continued production of these long after other manufacturers had ceased.

The first figure recorded in the existing pattern books was a smiling policeman directing traffic (303). This is an isolated model as the majority of the figures in the 1930s and 40s portrayed children, mostly modelled by Miss Greaves.

During World War Two Beswick introduced their Kindergarten series, copies of the popular Hummel style figures made in Germany by Goebbels. Beswick exported most of these pieces to America and Canada but, after the war, when Germany was again able to export, Beswick ceased production. As they were produced only throughout the war years, these pieces are now very rare. The original Hummel model number for each figure is recorded in the lists.

This cute style of figure was revived briefly in 1969 when Arthur Hallam modelled a series of doll-like children based upon drawings in a book by Joan Welsh Anglund, entitled, **A Friend Is Someone Who Loves You**, first published in 1959.

In the opinion of many collectors the finest Beswick figures are those designed by Miss Granoska between 1951 and 1954. Most portray characters in national costume, often accompanied by animals. One set depicts obstinate donkeys and goats carrying panniers of apples and grapes, being led, pushed or ridden by European peasants, whilst another group features national dancers of the world.

During the 1950s a number of figures appeared on horse-back, ranging from Colin Melbourne's stylised clowns riding bare-back to more realistic portraits of huntsmen and soldiers in the saddle. The latter are classed under the horses group.

Beswick have also produced many figures inspired by characters from film and literature and these are listed in their appropriate section.

Model No	Name of Model	Height inches	Value £	Design Date	Withdrawn By
303	Policeman on base	—	150-175	1935	1954
374	Girl tasting honey on base	5	150-175	1936	1954
375	Boy on base	—	150-175	1936	1954
388	Girl — finger in mouth	5¾	150-175	1936	1954
389	Man on rock	—	150-175	1936	1954
390	Girl in breeze on base	6	150-175	1936	1954
391	Girl with hands in muff	—	150-175	1936	1954
392	Child lying down	—	150-175	1936	1954
437	Girl with flared dress	4¾	150-175	1936	1954
438	Girl	—	150-175	1936	1954
441	Lady standing on base	—	150-175	1936	1954
442	Man standing on base	—	150-175	1936	1954
443	Child sitting	—	150-175	1936	1954
501	Clown	—	150-175	1937	1954

Anglund Children

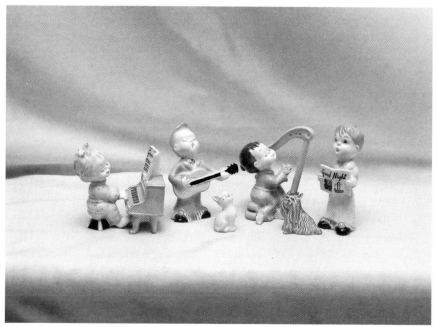

Bedtime Chorus

622	Mr Chamberlain	—	100-150	1938	1954
751	Boy Soldier in front of sentry box (bookends)	—	60-80	1939	1954
903	Bugle Boy (Hummel 97)	6	150-175	1940	1948
904	Book Worm (Hummel 3)	5	150-175	1940	1948
905	Goose Girl (Hummel 47)	6¼	150-175	1940	1948
906	Strolling Along (Hummel 5)	4¾	150-175	1941	1948
908	Stormy Weather (Hummel 71)	6	150-175	1941	1948
909	Puppy Love (Hummel 1)	5¼	150-175	1941	1948
910	Meditation (Hummel 13)	5	150-175	1941	1948
911	Max & Moritz (Hummel 123)	5¾	150-175	1941	1948
912	Farm Boy (Hummel 66)	6	150-175	1941	1948
913	Globe Trotter (Hummel 109)	5	150-175	1941	1948
914	Shepherd's Boy (Hummel 64)	4¼	150-175	1941	1948
924	Winston Churchill waving hat	—	200-250	1941	1954
940	A.R.P. Warden outside shelter, on one side; boy, girl & mother looking out on other.	—	150-175	1941	1954
952	Army Co-operation. Couple embracing on one side, soldier pulling pin from hand grenade on other	—	150-175	1941	1954
990	Boy strumming banjo	—	150-175	1942	1954
1010	Fairy Crying	6	200-250	1944	1954
1011	Fairy Drinking	4	200-250	1944	1954
1012	Fairy Sewing	4¾	200-250	1944	1954
1013	Fairy Baking	—	200-250	1944	1954
1020	Madonna	14	200-250	1945	1954
1086	Clown & Dog on base	7¼	150-175	1947	1965
1087	Jester sitting	—	150-175	1947	1965
1091	Gypsy Girl	7¼	150-175	1947	1965
1093	Hiker Boy	6	150-175	1947	1954
1094	Hiker Girl	6	150-175	1947	1954
1096	Sportsman	—	150-175	1947	1965
1097	Fruit Seller	—	150-175	1947	1965
1122	Butcher Boy with basket	5¾	150-175	1948	1965
1123	Man with flower pot	6¼	150-175	1948	1954
1124	Shepherd Boy with two sheep under arm	6¼	150-175	1948	1965
1125	Scotsman in kilt	6¼	150-175	1948	1954
1221	Hungarian Girl with turkey	7¼	150-175	1951	1965
1222	Polish Girl with hen	7	150-175	1951	1965
1223	Spaniard pulling donkey with panniers of apples	4½	200-250	1951	1965
1224	Spaniard pushing donkey with panniers of grapes	4½	200-250	1951	1965
1227	Swedish Girl holding cockerel	7	150-175	1952	1965
1230	Danish Girl leading pig	5¾	150-175	1952	1965
1234	Italian Girl leading goat	5½	200-250	1952	1965
1238	Italian Girl with goat eating hat	6	200-250	1952	1965
1244	Lady on donkey	5½	200-250	1952	1965
1245	Two children on donkey	4½	200-250	1952	1965

1247	Finnish Girl with duck	7	150-175	1952	1965
1262	Balinese Girl	3½	100-125	1952	1965
1263	Indian Girl	3½	100-125	1952	1965
1320	Siamese Dancer	3½	100-125	1953	1965
1321	Japanese Dancer	3½	100-125	1953	1965
1333	Chinese Dancer	3½	100-125	1954	1965
1334	Hawaiian Dancer	3½	100-125	1954	1965
1347	Susie Jamaica	7	200-250	1954	1975
1470	Clown on Horse (small) (CM series)	—	125-150	1957	1970
1476	Clown on horse (large) (CM series)	8½	150-175	1957	1970
1626	Toy drummer ⎫ coloured	2⅜	40-50	1959	1965
1627	Toy buglers ⎬ red and	2⅜	40-50	1959	1965
1628	Toy guards ⎭ blue	2⅜	40-50	1959	1965
1737	Man & Woman	—	150-200	1961	1970
1766	Road Gang: Foreman	—	40-50	1961	1965
1767	Road Gang: Digger	—	40-50	1961	1965
1768	Road Gang: Driller	—	40-50	1961	1965
1769	Road Gang: At Ease	—	40-50	1961	1965
1801/2	Pianist & Piano See also 1803 in Cats Section	3	60-80 each	1962	1969
1804	Boy without spectacles	3⅝	60-80	1962	1969
1805	Boy with spectacles See also 1824 in Dogs Section	3	60-80	1962	1969
1825	Boy with guitar	3	60-80	1962	1969
1826	Girl with harp	3⅝	60-80	1962	1969
1878	Welsh Lady	5	50-60	1963	1969
1937	Bust of Lady (C.M.C. on base)	6	50-60	1964	1965
1993	Lady with fan	7½	150-200	1964	1965
1994	Lady with hat	7½	150-200	1964	1965
1995	Lady in ball gown	7	150-200	1964	1965
2181	Knight of St John	6¾	150-175	1968	1969
2213	Bust of Shakespeare	3	25-35	1968	1973
2243	Bust of Shakespeare on pedestal (white)	5	30-40	1968	1973
2272	Anglund Boy	4⅜	100-125	1969	1971
2293	Anglund Girl	4⅜	100-125	1969	1971
2317	Anglund Girl	4¾	100-125	1969	1971

Bush Babies

Little Likeables (All models carry a John Beswick backstamp)

This collection of bone china animals, sculptures from the John Beswick Studio of Royal Doulton, broke new ground when they were first announced in the January 1985 price list.

All white, with a minimum of gold and pastel colouring, they immediately set new standards for the Beswick animal studies and had an irresistable charm of their own.

They were never illustrated in any form of catalogue, other than trade issues and so very little is known about them.

The series is very collectable and extremely well modelled by Robert Tabbenor and Diane Griffiths and should be on the "shopping list" of every dedicated Beswick collector.

By the end of 1986 they were beginning to be difficult to find and when the January 1987 price list was issued, the reason became clear, they had been withdrawn!

Each model was individually priced in an attractive gift box and prices ranged betweed £10 and £15.

The following collectors list gives all the information known about each model.

Model No	Name of Model	Height inches	Modeller	Value £'s
LL1	"Family gathering" (Hen and 2 chicks)	4½	Diane Griffiths	20-25
LL2	"Watching The World Go By" (Frog)	3¾	Robert Tabbenor	25-30
LL3	"Hide and Sleep" (Pig and 2 piglets)	3¼	Robert Tabbenor	20-25
LL4	"My Pony" (Pony)	7¼	Diane Griffiths	25-30
LL5	"On Top Of The World" (Elephant)	3¾	Diane Grffiths	20-25
LL6	"Treat Me Gently" (Fawn)	4½	Diane Griffiths	20-25
LL7	"Out At Last" (Duckling)	3¼	Robert Tabbenor	20-25
LL8	"Cats Chorus"	4¾	Robert Tabbenor	20-25

Studio Sculptures

This range of animal and bird studies was created by Design Manager Harry Sales and introduced in January 1985.

A new bonded ceramic body was used, which has the ability of capturing all the minute detail of each subject and literally brings it to life in a three-dimensional re-creation of the original drawing.

The initial sculpture entails a great deal of intricate modelling to achieve this and it is the final hand decoration on the finished product which really brings each sculpture to life.

Each item was separately boxed in specially designed packaging and some were available on polished hardwood bases.

Unfortunately the series has now been discontinued and individual pieces will therefore be very hard to find.

The shortest production runs were of model numbers 26 to 30 (inclusive) which were only available for six months.

A green baize is applied to the whole of the base on each model and an adhesive label is then applied on top of this, giving model details.

It should be noted that model numbers 23 to 25 (inclusive) were not produced.

Model No	Name of Model	Size inches	Introduced	Withdrawn	Value £'s
BEATRIX POTTER SERIES					
SS1	Timmy Willie	4¼	1/85	12/85	25-30
*SS2	Flopsy Bunnies	5	1/85	12/85	30-35
*SS3	Mr Jeremy Fisher	4	1/85	12/85	45-50
*SS4	Peter Rabbit	7	1/85	12/85	45-50
*SS11	Mrs Tiggy Winkle	5	1/85	12/85	45-50
SS26	Yock Yock (in the tub)	1⅞	1/86	6/86	45-50
SS27	Peter Rabbit (in the watering can)	3¼	1/86	6/86	45-50

* on wood base

Model No	Name of Model	Size inches	Introduced	Withdrawn	Value £'s
YOUNG FRIENDS SERIES					
SS5	"Puppy Love" (one dog washing another) black & brown, also black & white	4½	1/85	12/85	35-40
SS6	"I Spy" (two kittens in basket) available in tabby or white	4½	1/85	12/85	35-40
SS16	"Menu For Today" (puppy and kitten with cat food) brown & white or brown & tabby	3½	1/85	12/85	35-40
SS17	"Sharing" (dog & cat with bowl of milk)	3½	1/85	12/85	40-45

COUNTRYSIDE SERIES

SS8	"Contentment" (brown & white rabbit & young) also available in black & white	4¾	1/85	12/85	30-35
SS9	"Bright Eyes" (brown rabbit) also in black	4½	1/85	12/85	30-35
SS10	"Mind How You Go" (goose & goslings)	5¼	1/85	12/85	40-45
*SS13	"Happy Landing" (swan)	5	1/85	12/85	45-50
SS14	"The Chase" (3 dogs scrambling over a wall)	—	1/85	12/85	40-45
*SS15	"Hide and Seek" (3 dogs playing in a rock pool)	4½	1/85	12/85	40-45
SS18	"Planning Ahead" (squirrel with nuts)	3	1/85	12/85	25-30
SS19	"Early Bird" (wren)	2½	6/85	12/85	25-30
SS20	Golden Retriever	—	1/85	12/85	40-45
SS21	Pointer	—	6/85	12/85	40-45
SS22	English Setter	—	6/85	12/85	40-45
SS28	Robin	2¾	1/86	6/86	25-30
SS29	Blue Tit	2¾	1/86	6/86	25-30
SS30	Chaffinch	2¾	1/86	6/86	25-30

THELWELL SERIES

SS7	"I forgive you" (in grey or bay)	4	1/85	12/85	45-50
SS12	"Early Bath" (in grey or bay)	4¾	1/85	12/85	45-50

*on wood base

L—R **1263** *Indian Dancer;* **1333** *Chinese Dancer;* **1321** *Javanese Dancer*

Wall Plaques and Masks
(All models carry a Beswick backstamp)

Between the wars there was a rather bizarre fashion for adorning the living room walls with pottery portraits of chic young ladies or colourful characters. The Beswick artists catered for this trend between 1934 and 1939 and in that time produced no less than twenty different models. Varying in size between three and twelve inches, these wall masks were described as novelties in the catalogues and were available in assorted colourways, including a matt white glaze finish, at between two and three shillings each (10p and 15p). The fashionable ladies and cute little girls seem to have been the most popular and the modeller, Miss Greaves, has portrayed them with the very latest accessories, jaunty berets or cloche hats.

Appealing to a different taste were the character masks featuring either a Jester, an Indian, a Patriotic Soldier or the favourite Dickens characters Tony Weller and MrMicawber. On the reverse of Mr Micawber, the eternal optimist, is his famous line "until something turns up, I have nothing to bestow but advice'.' The Dickens subjects were the speciality of Mr Watkin who later modelled the same personalities in the form of character jugs.

Human faces were not the only subjects considered suitable for wall plaques; Beswick also produced bas-relief galleons and yachts, baskets of flowers, butterflies and the famous flights of birds. So distinctive are they that they have been catalogued in a section of their own.

Model No	Name of Model	Height inches	Value £	Design Date	Withdrawn By
197	Girl with beret	6	75-100	1934	1940
263	Galleon	10	75-100	1934	1940
274	Tony Weller	7½	75-100	1934	1940
277	Lady with beret in profile	—	150-200	1934	1940
279	Jester	5¼	75-100	1934	1940
280	Mr Micawber	9	75-100	1934	1940
282	Indian	7½	75-100	1934	1940
314	Girl with curly hair & beret	9½	150-200	1934	1940
362	Girl with beret & scarf	—	150-200	1935	1940
363	Lady with beret & scarf in profile	—	150-200	1935	1940
364	Girl with beret & pom-pom	—	150-200	1935	1940
365	Girl with beret	—	150-200	1935	1940
366	Girl with hat	—	150-200	1935	1940
367	Lady with hat & scarf in profile	—	150-200	1935	1940
380	Girl with hat	9½	150-200	1936	1940
393	Girl with plait	8½	150-200	1936	1940
419	Floral wall hoop	12	60-80	1936	1940
420	Floral wall triangle	—	60-80	1936	1940
436	Lady with beads	12	200-250	1936	1940
449	Lady with hat & spotted scarf	12½	200-300	1936	1940
457	Genie	9¼	150-175	1936	1940
483	Girl	9	150-200	1937	1940
507	The Gleaners	11	125-150	1937	1940

508	The Angelus	11	125-150	1937	1940
551	Basket of Flowers	10	75-100	1937	1940
556	Basket of Flowers	10½	75-100	1937	1940
557	Bowl of Flowers	6½	75-100	1937	1940
564	Bullrushes Plaque	—	75-100	1937	1940
565	Bowl of Flowers	5½	75-100	1937	1940
571	Bowl of Flowers	—	75-100	1937	1940
612	Boy with red hair	7¼	150-175	1938	1940
710	Lovers	8	75-100	1939	1940
714	Three Cherubs 'Hear No Evil' Etc	6 x 4½	100-125	1939	1940
715	'A World Without Friends Would Be Like A Garden Without Flowers'	9½ x 7½	125-150	1939	1940
719	'One of the Best'	9½ x 7½	125-150	1939	1940
723	'Those Who Bring Sunshine To The Lives Of Others Cannot Keep It From Themselves'	9½ x 7½	125-150	1939	1940
724	'Don't Worry It May Never Happen'	—	125-150	1939	1940
739	'Life's a Melody If You'll Only Hum the Tune'	—	125-150	1939	1940
740	'When You Are Up to Your Neck in Hot Water Think of the Kettle and Sing'	—	125-150	1939	1940
741	Lovers	—	75-100	1939	1945
764	Soldier	—	65-75	1939	1945
837	Plain Plaque	16 dia	40-50	1940	1954
839	Bird Plaque	16 dia	40-50	1940	1954
842	Gargoyle Mask	4½ x 5½	60-80	1940	1945
1632	Yacht No. 2242	7¾	50-75	1959	1965

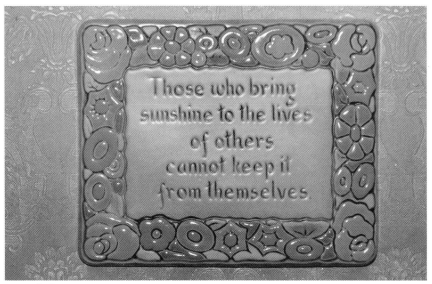

723 Wall Plaque

Part Three: Decorative Wares

(All models carry a Beswick backstamp, except 1988 re-introductions for Whyte & Mackay. Since 1988 they are marked Royal Doulton)

Advertising Ware

China and earthenware are ideal advertising media. They are durable, easy to clean and before the advent of plastic, they dominated the shop shelves.

Even today, although they are usually more expensive to produce than plastic they are still the chosen promotional tools for many breweries and distillers, who argue that a finely modelled ceramic decanter is less likely to be thrown away than a plain glass bottle and so their advertisement is more enduring. For over twenty years Beswick have been responsible for the figurative whisky containers, many in the form of animals, for Peter Thomson of Perth and most of these are still being made today. Beswick have recently revived their association with Bass by re-issuing the Lord Mayor jug first produced in 1961.

Double Diamond was the first beer to be promoted by Beswick and the brewer's well-known city gent character was modelled as a teapot in 1958, followed by a jug and a wall-plaque in 1960. Other familiar pub artifacts of this period include the Babycham fawn and the Courage cockerel. However, Beswick did not only cater for the spirit trade, their first recorded advertising piece was for Heatmaster who made teapots encased in thermal jackets. For this firm they made a liqueur set with the decanter in the form of a friar. It is not known what connection was intended between the liqueur container and Heatmaster's products, other than that they are all warming!

One of the most unusual advertising pieces in the collection features a little cobbler stitching a shoe which was made to celebrate Timpson's centenary in 1965.

Model No	Name of Model	Height inches	Value £	Design Date	Withdrawn By
1201	Friar Liqueur Set comprising tray & six measures for Heatmaster	8¼	60-80	1950	1973
1517	Double Diamond man container	8	80-100	1958	1970
1544	Barrel Lamp with tap	—	60-80	1958	1970
1587	Small Barrel (Sherry)	4¼	30-40	1959	1965
1598	Large Barrel (Port)	5	30-40	1959	1965
1615	Babycham Fawn	4	30-40	1959	1974
1616	Cockerel Courage Ales flask	—	100-125	1959	1965
1625	Woodbine ash tray	—	20-25	1959	1965

1672	Double Diamond face jug Two sizes	$6\frac{1}{2}$	100-125	1960	1965
1679	Double Diamond Public House Plaque	$8\frac{3}{4}$ x 10W	125-150	1960	1970
1680	Double Diamond man Plaque	$5\frac{1}{4}$ x $5\frac{1}{4}$	75-100	1960	1970
1681	Double Diamond dog Plaque	$4\frac{3}{4}$ L x $1\frac{3}{4}$	50-75	1960	1970
1741/1	Lord Mayor water jug (red bottle top)	$8\frac{1}{2}$	50-60	1961	1967
1741/2	Lord Mayor water jug (green bottle top)	$8\frac{1}{2}$	35-40	1986	1987
1820	Barrel B	$2\frac{1}{8}$	5-10	1962	1986
1829	Catto's Sportsman figure	$11\frac{1}{2}$	150-200	1962	1965
1850	Double Diamond lamp	$6\frac{1}{8}$	25-30	1962	1965
1856	Double Diamond dish	—	15-20	1962	1965
1869	Dubonnet stand	$7\frac{1}{2}$ x $4\frac{1}{4}$	20-25	1963	1970
1870	Dubonnet bottle	$5\frac{1}{2}$	20-25	1963	1970
1871	Dubonnet poodle	$4\frac{1}{8}$	60-80	1963	1967
1872	Dubonnet bulldog	$3\frac{3}{4}$	60-80	1963	1967
1946	Timpsons the shoemaker dish	$3\frac{1}{2}$	40-50	1964	1966
1955	Smiths Crisps Plaque	$7\frac{1}{4}$ x 2	35-45	1964	1970
1983	Canada Dry ash tray	9	20-25	1964	1967
1984	Rothmans lamp	$4\frac{1}{2}$	25-30	1964	1967
1990	Dulux dog	$12\frac{1}{2}$	250-300	1964	1970
1999	Bath oil bottle & stopper for Cussons	$7\frac{1}{2}$	10-15	1966	1967
2000	Covered bath salt jar for Cussons	$5\frac{1}{4}$	10-15	1966	1967
2001	Bourne & Hollingsworth ash tray	8 x $6\frac{1}{2}$	20-25	1964	1967
2009	Skol lamp	6	25-30	1965	1968
2010	Double Diamond lamp	$5\frac{1}{2}$	25-30	1965	1968
2011	Skol lamp	6	25-30	1965	1968
2018	Double Diamond lamp	$5\frac{1}{2}$	25-30	1965	1968
2033	Fishermans flask B	$3\frac{3}{4}$	10-15	1965	1970
2047	Gallagher ash bowl	9x 7	20-25	1965	1970
2048	Les Leston steering wheel ash bowl	7 $\frac{1}{4}$	30-40	1965	1967
*2051	Nessie (Loch Ness Monster) B, 2 models; one with head stopper one with base stopper	3	5-10	1965	1986
2052	Piccadilly ash tray	$8\frac{1}{8}$	20-25	1965	1970
2053	Gallagher water jug	$5\frac{3}{8}$	25-30	1965	1970
2055	Craven A oval ash tray	11 x $6\frac{5}{8}$	20-25	1966	1970
2056	Pheasant flask B	$3\frac{1}{2}$	10-15	1966	1970
2057	Pike flask B	$3\frac{1}{2}$	10-15	1966	1970
2058	Deer flask B	$3\frac{1}{2}$	10-15	1966	1970
2060	Hunts (lady rider on horse jumping fence) Plaque	$7\frac{3}{8}$	125-150	1966	1970
2076	Robert Burns cottage flask B	$3\frac{1}{2}$	10-15	1966	1971
2077	Edinburgh Castle flask B	$3\frac{1}{2}$	10-15	1966	1970
2079	Watneys Plaque	$6\frac{1}{4}$	35-45	1966	1970
2086	Beswick Plaque (Black & Gold)	$2\frac{1}{2}$	15-20	1966	1980

Catto's Sportsman Figure

2088	Peters Griffin Woodward bust USA dept. store	$3\frac{1}{2}$	50-60	1967	1970
2092	Peters Griffin Woodward character jug USA dept. store	5	75-100	1967	1970
*2104	Eagle flask B	$4\frac{3}{8}$	5-10	1967	1986
2115	Pall Mall ash tray	$9\frac{3}{4} \times 4\frac{3}{4}$	20-25	1967	1969
2180	Tower Bridge flask	$3\frac{1}{2}$	10-15	1968	1971
2185	Arundel Castle flask	$4\frac{1}{2}$	10-15	1968	1971
2192	Benson & Hedges square ash tray	5	20-25	1968	1975
2206	Deer flask	$3\frac{1}{2}$	10-15	1968	1975
2207	Trout flask	$3\frac{1}{2}$	10-15	1968	1975
2208	Pheasant flask	$3\frac{1}{2}$	10-15	1968	1975
2218	Benson & Hedges orb ash tray	7 D	20-25	1968	1975
2219	Craven A ash tray	8 D	20-25	1968	1970
2237	Babycham concave Plaque	$6\frac{1}{4} \times 3\frac{3}{8}$	50-60	1968	1975
2241	Hamlet ash tray	$7\frac{1}{2} \times 5$	20-25	1968	1975
2260	Bemax jar & lid	—	25-30	1969	1970
2261	Hamlet cigars ash tray	$6\frac{1}{8} \times 6$	20-25	1969	1975
2280	Chante Clair cockerel jug	$9\frac{3}{4}$	100-150	1969	1971
2281	Golden Eagle flask B	$10\frac{7}{8}$	45-60	1969	1984
2318	Golf Ball flask B	$1\frac{5}{8}$ D	10-15	1970	1986
2349	Robert Burns flask B	—	50-75	1970	1975
**2350	Haggis flask B	$2\frac{1}{2}$	5-10	1971	1986
2486	Bass Charrington (young couple behind letter E)	9	75-100	1973	1976
2487	Bass Charrington (rugby players behind letter E)	9	75-100	1973	1976
2488	Bass Charrington (squire & friend behind letter E)	9	75-100	1973	1976
2506	Bass Charington (Minton ewer jug)	$6\frac{3}{4}$	35-45	1974	1976
2514	White Horse whisky (horse)	$6\frac{3}{4}$	200-250	1974	1976
2518	Worthington (butcher & baker behind letter E)	9	100-125	1974	1976
2519	Worthington (woman & dog behind letter E)	9	100-125	1974	1976
2520	Worthington (parson & policeman behind letter E)	9	100-125	1974	1976
2561	Grouse for Mathew Gloag Ltd	$9\frac{3}{8}$	75-85	1976	1984
*2583	Osprey flask B	$7\frac{3}{4}$	40-60	1977	1986
**2636	Squirrel flask B	$3\frac{1}{2}$	10-15	1978	1986
*2639	Kestrel flask B	$6\frac{1}{2}$	40-60	1979	1986
*2640	Buzzard flask B	$6\frac{1}{2}$	40-60	1979	1986
*2641	Merlin flask B	$6\frac{1}{2}$	40-60	1979	1986
*2642	Peregrine flask B	$6\frac{1}{2}$	40-60	1979	1986
2670	Bunratty castle (5000 edition)	6	40-60	1980	1983
*2678	Golden Eagle flask B	$10\frac{1}{2}$	50-60	1984	1987
**2686	Otter flask B	$2\frac{1}{4}$	10-15	1981	1986
**2687	Badger flask B	3	10-15	1981	1986

*Re-introduced 1987 for Whyte & Mackay(Glasgow), now current and carrying the Royal Doulton backstamp
** Re-introduced 1987-1991 for Whyte & Mackay

**2693	Seal flask B	3⅞	10-15	1981	1986
*2781	Tawny Owl flask B	6¼	40-60	1986	1987
*2809	Barn Owl flask B	6¾	40-60	1986	1987
*2825	Short Eared Owl flask B	6½	40-60	1986	1987
2826/1	Snowy Owl flask B	5¾	50-60	1986	1987
*2826/2	Snowy Owl flask W&M	6½	40-60	1986	1986

B = Beneagles whisky container for Peter Thomson (Perth) Ltd.
D= diameter
*Re-introduced 1987 for Whyte & Mackay(Glasgow), now current and carrying the Royal Doulton backstamp
** Re-introduced 1987-1991 for Whyte & Mackay

2376 *Christmas 1972 Plaque*

Christmas Around the World
(All carry the Beswick mark)

There are a growing number of collectors who seem to enjoy Christmas all year long by tracking down pieces with colourful, seasonal imagery. The fashion for collecting plates with a Christmas theme developed in the USA and it was originally for an American audience that Beswick introduced a series of annual plates depicting 'Christmas Around the World'. In order to convey the distinctive traditions of festivities in other lands, several different artists were invited to contribute to this collection and their artwork was then modelled in low relief by Beswick artists. Harry Sales, the company's design manager, visualised the first, 'Old England' in 1972. Chavela Castrejon was commissioned to design 'Christmas in Mexico' issued in 1973 and Dimitri Yordanov was responsible for 'Christmas in Bulgaria' for the 1974 plate. The remaining four plates were all designed by Alton Toby, his final scene of 'Christmas in America' completing the set of seven in 1978.

In addition to these plates, the Beswick artists experimented with a few relief modelled rectangular plaques portraying yuletide scenes in Dickensian mood but it would appear these did not go into production in any great quantity.

Plates & Plaques

Model No	Description	Size inches	Value £'s	Plate or Plaque	Issue Date
2376	Christmas 1972	11¼ x 5½	175-200	Plaque	1972
2393	Christmas in England	8 x 8	35-40	Plate	1972
2419	Christmas in Mexico	8 x 8	35-40	Plate	1973
2430	Christmas 1973	11¼ x 5½	175-200	Plaque	1973
2443	Regent Street	11 x 7	125-150	Plaque	1973
2444	Christmas Ornament		75-80	Plaque	1973
2462	Christmas in Bulgaria	8 x 8	30-35	Plate	1974
2522	Christmas in Norway	8 x 8	30-35	Plate	1975
2538	Christmas in Holland	8 x 8	30-35	Plate	1976
2567	Christmas in Poland	8 x 8	30-35	Plate	1977
2598	Christmas in America	8 x 8	35-40	Plate	1978

Christmas Carol Tankards

(All carry the Beswick Mark)

Dickens also provided the inspiration for the limited edition collection of tankards launched in 1971. Each year a scene from his classic **A Christmas Carol** was vividly modelled in low relief and admirably captured the spirit of the traditional English yuletide. The set of twelve was completed in 1982 and although the edition size was published as 15,000 each year, it is believed that the final number produced was less than this, with most going to the United States, Canada and Australia. However, the British collector can still find them at antique fairs and markets.

Model No	Description	Value £	Issue Date
2351	Cratchit & Scrooge	50-55	1971
2375	Carolers	50-55	1972
2423	Solicitation	50-55	1973
2445	Marley's Ghost	45-50	1974
2523	Ghost of Christmas Past	45-50	1975
2539	Ghost of Christmas Present	45-50	1976
2568	Ghost of Christmas Present	45-50	1977
2599	Ghost of Christmas Present	50-55	1978
2624	Ghost of Christmas Future	50-55	1979
2657	Scrooge Visits His Own Grave	50-55	1980
2692	Scrooge Going to Church	50-55	1981
2764	Christmas at Bob Cratchit's	55-60	1982

1235 Barracuda

Commemoratives (All carry the Beswick mark)

Royal Commemoratives produced by Beswick form a small but interesting collection. Like other pottery companies Beswick issued pieces to commemorate the coronation of HRH Edward VIII but when he suddenly abdicated on December 10 1936, new wares featuring HRH George VI had to be prepared.

As well as two mugs, of which one was musical, Beswick obtained the reproduction rights for a collection of souvenirs modelled by Felix Weiss. These unusual commemoratives all depicted the bust of George VI and are listed below.

The next Royal coronation was that of HRH Elizabeth II in 1953 and the selection of mugs and trays issued for this occasion are also detailed below.

Model No	Name of Model	Value £	Design Date	Withdrawn By
377	Edward VIII Plaque	60-80	1936	1937
445	Edward VIII Coronation tankard	30-40	1936	1937
446	Edward VIII Coronation mug	15-20	1936	1937
451	Edward VIII bust	60-80	1936	1937
458	Edward VIII vase	60-80	1936	1937
461	George VI Coronation musical mug	75-100	1937	1938
462	George VI Coronation mug	15-20	1937	1938
468	George VI bust	60-80	1937	1938
469	George VI bust	50-60	1937	1938
470	George VI plaque	60-80	1937	1938
471	George VI plaque	50-60	1937	1938
472	George VI bookend	50-60	1937	1938
1250	Elizabeth II Coronation mug	15-20	1952	1954
1251	Elizabeth II Coronation beaker	15-20	1952	1954
1252	Elizabeth II Embossed Coronation mug	20-25	1952	1954
1253	Elizabeth II Coronation tray (large)	20-25	1952	1954
1254	Elizabeth II Coronation tray (small)	15-20	1952	1954

Shakespeare Series Ware (All carry the Beswick mark)

The plays of William Shakespeare (1564-1616) have been a fertile source of inspiration for Beswick artists. Mr Hallam, Mr Gredington and Mr Orwell have interpreted some of the most famous scenes in a series of jugs, tankards and mugs, superbly modelled in low relief. **Romeo and Juliet**, Shakespeare's first tragedy and perhaps his best known work, is represented by a jug and a wall plaque both depicting the fond farewell. The other plaque in the series features characters from the famous comedy **As You Like It** and the quotation "That would I, were I of all kingdoms king". Suitable inscriptions appear on all the Shakespeare wares. Hamlet's famous soliloquy "To be or not to be" is inscribed on a tankard depicting a scene from the play and a jug features the Prince of Denmark with his father's ghost and the quotation "Hamlet — be thou a spirit of health?" Sir John Falstaff, Shakespeare's jovial knight also features on both a jug and a tankard. He was so popular with audiences in the sixteenth century that he appears in **Henry IV** Part I, **Henry V** and later in **The Merry Wives of Windsor**.

All these Shakespearean wares so far discussed are relatively easy to find today but the last two depicting scenes from **A Midsummer Night's Dream** which were added to the set in 1955, can be quite elusive.

Model No	Name of Model	Height inches	Value £	Design Date	Withdrawn By
1126	Falstaff jug	8	75-100	1948	1973
1127	Falstaff tankard	4	20-25	1948	1973
1146	Hamlet jug	8¼	75-100	1949	1973
1147	Hamlet tankard	4¼	20-25	1949	1973
1209	As You Like It wall plaque	12 dia	100-125	1950	1969
1210	Romeo & Juliet wall plaque	12 dia	100-125	1951	1969
1214	Juliet jug	8¼	60-80	1951	1973
1215	Juliet mug	4	20-25	1951	1973
1366	A Midsummer Night's Dream — jug	8	125-150	1955	1973
1368	Midsummer Night's Dream — mug	4¼	50-75	1955	1973

Trentham Art Wares

During the 1930s a seven year agreement was made between Beswick and Hardy, a wholesaler based in Nottingham, for items to be designed and produced at Beswick, but to be marketed under the name of 'Trentham Art Wares'.

Approximately two hundred different items were produced and marked with the Beswick model number and 'Made in England' impressed on the base together with the 'Trentham Art Wares' backstamp. Most pieces were vases or jugs but there were approximately thirty animals, figures or birds and it is likely that these only carried the backstamp.

The agreement lapsed in 1941 and Beswick were then free to continue production of the more popular items, but carrying only their own backstamp or impressed mark.

Several of these pieces continued in production until the mid sixties and the following list gives all known model numbers which were subject to this agreement.

Model Numbers

21-48	380/84/85	653-657	902-914
76/77	422/24/28	668	918-922
79-81	431/32/34/35	675-680	955-959
91/94/95/98	439/40	688	987
129-132	444	693/94/99	
136	447-449	700/02	
140	490/92/94/95/96	731	
148-167	498-500	760-62/65	
289-292	503-505	770-784	
299-301	546-548	800-809	
306/07	550/52/54/55	813/15/19	
345-357	558/60/62/63	827/29	
362-367	566/68-70	836/38	
373/79	573		

Britannia Collection (All backstamped Beswick)

This range of ceramic studies is taken from the existing Beswick collection, with the exception of the Special Commission Unicorn, and is finished in a rich bronze glaze with subtle shading. This new decorative process was developed by Graham Tongue, Design Manager of the John Beswick Studio.

Model No	Name of Model	Height inches	Value £	Introduction Date	Withdrawn By
868	Huntsman	10	85·00	1989	C
*981	Stag (small)	9	29·95	1989	C
1018	Bald Eagle	7¼	45·00	1989	C
*2542	Hereford Bull	7½	119·00	1989	C
*2549	Polled Hereford Bull	6¼	59·95	1989	C
2629	Stag (large)	13½	129·00	1989	C
*2688	Spirit of the Wind (horse)	9	45·00	1989	C
2760	Pheasant	10½	199·00	1989	C
*2914	Spirit of Earth (shire horse)	8½	45·00	1989	C
*2986	Setter	8½	49·95	1989	C
*3011	Pointer	8⅜	49·95	1989	C
*3021	Unicorn	9	49·95	1989	C
*3066	Retriever	7½	49·95	1989	C

*on ceramic base

1266 Large-mouthed Black Bass

Miscellaneous Wares (All backstamped Beswick)

This section is intended to cover those items which do not easily fit into a set category.

Earlier pieces, in particular, will be very hard to find and may also have no Beswick mark.

There will also be variations in colour and markings on the yacht series and also the fish trays and dishes have an external stoneware finish and a gloss centre.

Model No	Name of Model	Height inches	Value £	Design Date	Withdrawn By
253	Shakespeare House Cruet set and base	3¼	30-35	1934	1971
278	Mosque Cruet set & base		40-45	1934	1954
284	Lady Napkin Ring		75-100	1934	1940
311	Duck Napkin Ring		25-30	1934	1940
312	Rabbit Napking Ring		25-30	1934	1940
313	Frog Napkin Ring		25-30	1934	1940
376	Rabbit Place Card Holder	2¼	40-45	1936	1954
460	Rowing Boat Cruet Dutch Lady & Man S&P plus Captain Mustard		50-60	1936	1954
576	Motor Coach teapot		60-80	1938	1954
609	3 piece Chess cruet & stand		50-60	1938	1954
613	Soldier cruet set		50-60	1938	1954
945	Aeroplane (twin engine)		40-50	1941	1954
1045	Robert Burns jug	8	100-125	1946	1967
1099	Cock & Hen S&P	2	25-30	1947	1965
1273	Childrens Tea Set		100-125	1952	1954
1304	Fish shaped pin tray	3 long	10-15	1953	1969
1596	Robert Burns mug	4¼	50-75	1959	1967
1610	Yacht Table model "Firefly"	5½	75-100	1959	1965
1633	Yacht Table model G.P.14	11	125-150	1959	1965
1634	Yacht Table model "Heron"	8⅜	100-125	1959	1965
1760	Pig head money box	8½	50-75	1961	1967
1761	Fox head money box	8½	50-75	1961	1967
2128	Fish ash tray	7 long	15-20	1967	1971
2129	Whale ash tray	7¼ long	15-20	1967	1971
2133	Fish ash tray	9½	15-20	1967	1971
2156	Cat Pepper	5½	20-25	1967	1969
2157	Cat Salt	5½	20-25	1967	1969
2167	Fish Dish (shows bones)	7½ x 6	15-20	1967	1971
2169	Seahorse ash tray	10½	15-20	1967	1971
2170	Fish Dish (shows bones)	7⅝ x 5⅜	15-20	1967	1971
2171	Fish Dish (shows bones)	12 x 4⅛	15-20	1967	1971
2199	Cockerel ash tray	8 long	15-20	1968	1971
2209	Pheasant ash tray	12¾	15-20	1968	1971

Catalogue Specials

Since 1987 a number of current items have been mounted on ceramic bases, for direct purchase from mail order catalogues.

Most had a polished brass name-plate affixed to the base, with a suitably descriptive title. Now discontinued, they are an unusual addition to the Beswick collection, but do tend to take up a lot of space.

In addition, there was at least one example of a Shire horse (2914) being mounted on a ceramic base with a green top instead of the production "earth" colour.

This order was for an American TV station and all were sold in this way. The backstamp was circular and read "Beswick — Made in England".

Model No	Name-plate Title	Model names
1558/1678	"Watch It"	Siamese Cat/Mouse
2950/1436	"Good Friends"	Playful puppy "Nap Time"/Kitten
1460/1436	"Sharing"	Dachshund sitting/Kitten
818/1034	"Horses Great & Small"	Shire/Shetland foal
2267/2110	"Jenny's Baby"	Donkey/Donkey foal
1765/1828	"Ewe and I"	Sheep
1452/1453		Pigs
1886/3093	"Playtime"	Kitten/Ball of wool
1501/2262/		
2263	"Tally Ho!"	Huntsman and 2 Hounds